Getting Rich ~~Quick~~ The Right Way

The Complete Guide To Investing In Real Estate Right The First Time

By Ron Phillips

TABLE OF CONTENTS

Free Reader Bonus Material

As a thank you for your purchase, please visit the following link to claim special bonus content exclusively for our readers...

www.GetStartedInvestingNow.com

Getting Rich ~~Quick~~ The Right Way

Preface

About the Author

With nearly two decades of experience in the business, Ron Phillips has become an expert in helping others achieve their dream of financial stability. This knowledge, however, is not something which was developed over night. After spending thousands of dollars and countless hours on seminars and educational material, he realized why most people fail. The problem, as he saw it, is the gap between education and implementation.

There are many courses which claim to help students increase their wealth. These courses may be full of valuable information but they rarely go beyond basic education. Once the course is over, students are left completely alone. After seeing his fellow students consistently fail to make the money they wanted, he decided it was time to finally bridge that gap. His solution was the Wealth Accelerator System.

As CEO of the Wealth Accelerator System, Ron personally works with students from all walks of life. His goal is to both educate and guide his students down a path which will change their financial lives. He does this through seminars, videos, books and one on one mentoring in which he seeks to illustrate every step needed to secure a safe and profitable future. Over the years, his company has been able to help thousands of ordinary people begin living the life they deserve without the need to worry about financial resources.

Why He Wrote this Book

This book represents another step in Ron's quest to free people from financial concern. It was written to help bring this valuable information to an audience who may not be able to personally attend his classes and seminars. He wanted a way to reach out to those millions of individuals who are looking at their resources and seeing their dreams slip further and further away. He needed something which could be accessible, something which would fit into busy schedules and tight budgets.

More importantly, he wanted something which would allow people to learn at their own pace. The information contained in this book is laid out in such a way that nearly anyone, regardless of their financial experience, will be able to learn everything necessary to grow their personal wealth. This is a complete course, from start to finish. Once the book is over, readers will be able to begin achieving the same level of success enjoyed by thousands of Ron's students.

What you hold in your hands, however, is much more than a textbook. This is the physical embodiment of Ron's mission in life. After seeing countless people lose everything, after watching people's lifelong dreams come to a catastrophic end, Ron felt a moral obligation to help. It is this spirit of service which is the foundation of the Wealth Accelerator System. It is this desire to help others which truly sets his book apart from the rest. Ron Phillips' goal is not to get rich, he is not trying to become famous, he is simply trying to help other people free themselves from their financial burdens and secure a stable future for themselves and their families.

Who Should Read This Book

This book has been written for anyone who has ever worried about their future. We live in a world of dramatic market fluctuations, bad information and bubbles which seem to burst without warning. As inflation erodes the value of our money and income begins to stagnate, it can be far too easy to lose hope. Many people have worked their entire lives only to find they no longer have the resources needed to retire.

This is a book for people who are tired of being kept up at night by financial concerns. It is meant for people who are willing to make a few smart investments in their own future. While the information is highly detailed, it is not meant for financial experts alone. Nearly anyone with some common sense will be able to create a system of wealth acquisition regardless of their past experience. The truth is you simply do not need to be a guru to make money like one.

The one thing that a reader does need, however, is a strong desire to begin living the life they want. It does not matter if that life includes traveling the world, living in luxury homes or simply ensuring a stable and happy future for one's family. The only thing that is needed is the motivation to begin making the right choices and a determination to continue doing what must be done. Anyone who has experienced financial hardship should already have this drive.

Who Should NOT Read This Book

This book is not for anyone looking to simply "get rich quick." The system outlined in these pages, like most things in life, requires a bit of time to come to full fruition. Time is an investment. Every moment spent learning this system and understanding its concepts is another step towards success. Patience will be rewarded with an ability to develop your own wealth accumulating system and the confidence to know that each phase has been completed correctly.

While this system will allow for the creation of income streams which are almost entirely passive, there is still some work which needs to be done. This book has not been written for people who are unwilling to work towards their own success. Knowledge may be powerful but the willingness to take action is what separates those who are successful from those who continue to struggle. Fortunately, readers will not be left completely alone because Ron's business has been built around working directly with his students.

Just as this system requires an investment of time, there will also be a need to invest some money. This book is not meant for people who are looking to acquire wealth without the need to invest capital. No matter how someone makes their money, there will need to be some investment and this is simply a fact of life. This book will, however, offer a number of different methods for obtaining this investment capital. Due to the nature of the strategies outlined in these chapters, only a small amount of capital is needed to begin and that money is then returned as quickly as possible. In the end, this is a system which pays for itself.

Getting Rich ~~Quick~~ The Right Way

What You Will Learn And How You Will Learn It

This book will present a lot of information. Readers should be prepared for a dramatic shift in the way in which they think about money. One of the goals of this book is to help a person break out of the employee mindset, where their income is dependent on someone else, and begin thinking like someone who is financially independent. Over the course of this book, readers will learn about the following:

Real Estate Basics

Real estate can be a complicated subject. This section will illustrate, as clearly and simply as possible, the basics of real estate and how it can be used to generate wealth. The media has spent quite a bit of time demonizing real estate and its value as an investment. This portion will not only dispel these myths but explain how and why this is currently and historically one of the best investments in the world.

Readers will also begin to understand the differences in each type of real estate and why each one works. Ranging from raw land to fully developed and occupied properties, readers will be able to determine which type of property is best suited to their needs. This portion of the book will also detail the different ways in which real estate is used to create an incredible return as well as explaining the advantages and disadvantages of each method.

Income Producing Properties

Once the basics are out of the way, readers will develop an understanding of income producing properties. There are a number of different property types, which can produce a valuable income, and readers will learn about each one. Not every property is equal and this section will focus only on those types of properties which produce the best possible return.

The purpose of this section is to help readers develop the ability to recognize income producing properties and how to differentiate them from the rest. They will learn how and why a property produces income and what factors should be present before any investment is made.

Land

Land is the most basic of all real estate and it can also be the most valuable. Despite the great potential for profit, land is also one of the more difficult types of property to comprehend. This portion of the book will help readers understand how land produces a return, where to find it and what to look for. This is information which is rarely found elsewhere because so few people truly have any experience with it.

In addition to this, readers will also discover why now is absolutely the best time to use land as a key player in their wealth acquisition strategy. Despite the negative press, this type of property investment is set to be the most desirable and expensive asset available. In a very short period of time the prices of land will multiply in much the same way as gold.

Combining Land with Developed Properties

Combining land with developed and occupied properties is what makes this system so unique. Most investors will focus on either land or income producing properties but only a small fraction will combine them. This is due, in part, to the simple fact that most people fail to understand how this is done.

This combination creates a reciprocating strategy which not only pays for itself, but generates new income which can then be used to increase the profitability of the system as a whole. This technique will be explained in detail and readers will be privy to some of the most eye opening information they are likely to find anywhere.

How We Do It

The information presented in this book is not academic. This is a complete explanation of the way in which our company makes its money. Readers will be presented with real world examples from both other students and our own personal experience.

This is a unique opportunity to discover the secrets we have used over nearly two decades to not only grow our own bank accounts but to help others vastly increase their financial assets as well. This is the type of information which is closely guarded by other entities but we are making it available to those willing to take the time to read it.

Now is the Time

There is never any time like the present and this is particularly true for financial matters. We are currently at a very crucial point in the history of the financial world and action needs to be taken now, before the opportunities are gone. Read through these chapters, understand the system and take action as soon as possible. This is the key to financial success.

Getting Rich ~~Quick~~ The Right Way

Introduction

It seems as if everyone is intrigued by the prospect of investing. Most people work for a living and, while they may enjoy their job, they are constrained by this need for employment. Not only does a job require a large amount of time and dedication, there are very few opportunities to increase a job's financial benefits. Someone may work for a company for many years and only see a slight increase in their wages.

The alternative is investing. Investing allows us to utilize a relatively small amount of money to generate even more income. With a few smart purchases, money can be multiplied many times over. This is not to say investing and working are mutually exclusive. Many people, in fact, work a regular job and then invest their savings.

What makes investing truly attractive is the virtually unlimited potential for profit. A good investment can turn a small amount of money into a veritable fortune. Most people, however, are not even interested in becoming extraordinarily wealthy. They would simply like to make enough money to retire.

The Retirement Problem

Retirement is the goal for which many people are working. One day, they hope, they will be able to stop working and simply enjoy their lives. This requires a fair amount of money and many people will begin saving for retirement from an early age. They may currently be investing without even being aware of it through the use of an IRA, a retirement account which can often include a number of different investments.

The problem many people are running into, however, is their retirement plans have begun to fall apart. The current economic problems, coupled with the ever increasing cost of living, have eroded many retirement accounts. People who once thought they were close to this goal are now realizing they may never be able to stop working.

The root of this problem stems from an unstable financial climate. Financial markets have always fluctuated. There have been major shifts, such as The Great Depression but there have always been times of gain and times of loss. The truth about these markets is it is impossible to predict when these peaks and valleys will arise.

Recent History

We are currently suffering from the backlash of an economic downturn. Towards the end of the last century, people were making more money than ever before. The stock market was booming, property values were exploding and investing was a popular option. A few years later, in about 2008, the bubble had burst.

Property values began to drop. Stock prices fell significantly. The entire economy was taking a nosedive and there was nothing anybody could do about it. During this period, millions of dollars were lost. This affected both big Wall Street investors as well as the everyday, average American. Since so many retirement funds were tied to different investments, many people watched their savings dwindle away.

Economists had hoped things would turn around quickly but this was not the case. The entire country had lost so much money that people were afraid to start spending again. The economy stagnated while costs continued to increase. People who had, at one time, been very close to retirement were now dealing with the reality of working for at least another decade.

After a number of years, we are finally seeing the economy begin to rebound. It is happening slowly but it will speed up over time. The problem for many people, however, is they are still unable to retire. Worse yet, people who should be planning for retirement are afraid. Having watched people, just like themselves, lose everything through no fault of their own has frightened them.

The reality of our current situation is that people still want to retire. Everyone wants to be able to stop working and enjoy their life, secure in their finances. They simply do not know how to do this. There were traditional methods of planning for retirement but many of them proved to be unreliable. People do not want to work for decades, saving whenever they can, only to find their money is gone when they really need it.

The situation has gotten so dire, in fact, that many people have simply given up. They are dealing with the concept that they may never retire. They are no longer looking into retirement accounts, they are not saving and they certainly are not investing. The reason for this is they simply do not know what to do. They have no idea how to increase their own personal assets, other than working day after day.

Getting Rich ~~Quick~~ The Right Way

The Key

Investing is the key to retirement, now more than ever. The economy is different, however, and investing needs to be approached carefully. When they consider investing, most people will think of the stock market. Investing in stocks had once been a reliable and profitable way to multiply one's own financial resources but this is no longer the case.

Our world is connected like never before. Information travels faster than ever and an event in one part of the world is known all over the globe by the end of the day. What this means for investors is the stock market is more volatile than ever before. The value of a stock is heavily dependent on information. Since this information can change overnight, there is no telling what might happen to the value of a stock.

Product launches, for example, used to mean an increase in a company's stock prices. The internet, however, has given the consumer market the ability to instantly state their opinions on these new products. If one is poorly received, the consumer market will make it known immediately. This can cause the prices of that company's stocks to plummet.

In addition to this, many stable stocks increase at far too slow a rate. Some stocks may produce dividends but these are often far too low as well. With the value of the dollar decreasing through inflation and the cost of living continuing to increase, stocks are no longer the foundation of a stable financial future. While there is still money to be made in this market, it takes a near expert level of knowledge to make a significant amount of it.

A Better Way

This book is about finding a better way. It is about learning how to be smart with your money and put it to work for you. The goal of this book is to teach you our technique for wealth accumulation. This is a technique that we use ourselves and we have taught to thousands of other people over the years. Our purpose is to educate people so they can make their dreams of retirement a reality.

We do this through investing in real estate. Real estate has gotten a lot of bad publicity in recent years. It seems to be one of the media's favorite scapegoats. This is actually a recent occurrence because, for a few years, the media was hailing real estate as the solution to all of our financial woes. Once things started to change, however, the media began vilifying it.

This is because the media sells negative news. It is what they do best. The angle they choose for their stories is almost always negative and entirely pessimistic. The bottom line is the media does not really care about us, they are not trying to protect or educate us, they are simply selling advertising space. They will say and do whatever they can to increase their audience.

Real estate is, in reality, simply one of the best investments you can make. It is a far more stable and solid asset than a stock and it produces much more income than a savings account. Houses and land will never cease to be in demand. The prices for real estate may be low, right now, but they are guaranteed to increasing very quickly.

These low prices, in fact, are one of the reasons real estate is such a great investment. There are currently no other opportunities like this. Both houses and land are so undervalued that, given a little patience and the right system, it is nearly impossible to not make a profit on a real estate investment. Very soon, within the next two years at most, these values will rebound and the prices will go back to where they once were.

Our System

This book details our system. What we do is not real estate speculation. We do not flip or rehabilitate houses. We invest our money into a proven system which begins to pay for itself almost immediately. Given enough time, our system becomes an income-producing machine, which will increase your financial assets many times over.

This system is based on over 50 years' worth of experience in real estate and investing. This is not theory or conjecture, it is a method we have developed, tested and perfected. It has been scientifically designed to support itself and produce what is essentially an unlimited stream of income. This method is absolutely modern and has been created with our current economic situation in mind.

Over the course of the next few chapters, you will become an expert in our system. It does not matter if you have no experience with real estate, investing or finance at all. Our system is so simple and straightforward that you will learn everything you need to know in a very short period of time. In addition to this, we will provide you with all of the resources you need to get started.

We have created this system because we want to help others. Rather than keeping it a closely guarded secret, our intent has, from the beginning, been to teach this system to as many people as possible. This is something we have had to do rather quickly because time is running out. The incredible potential for wealth accumulation we have in our current economic climate is bound to change.

Before too long, property values are going to rise. People will soon be purchasing houses and developers will be buying land. The economy has already started to rebound so this boom is only a couple of years away at most. For us, and everyone who has discovered and followed our system, this will be a period of incredible abundance.

If you have been working hard your entire life then you are our ideal student. You owe it to yourself to find out how to begin accumulating your own personal wealth and secure your retirement. The following chapters will enlighten you to a new way of thinking about money. You will free yourself from the bonds of endless employment and gain the knowledge needed to live the life you deserve.

Imagine a future where money is no longer a concern. Picture yourself living freely, without worrying about your own financial future. Imagine having set up a system of wealth accumulation that is so easy to understand you will wonder why others refuse to pursue it.

This future is the end result of the journey you are about to begin right now.

Real Estate Basics

If you were to go out and ask a random selection of people for their opinion on real estate, nearly all of them will be negative. This is due, in part, to the media's portrayal of real estate in an extremely negative light. The problem is the media makes its living from selling negative news.

People tune in to hear about accidents, crimes and catastrophes. Any positive news is generally saved for the end of the program and is quickly forgotten by the audience. If, however, these people understood a little about the history of real estate, they might change their minds.

A Recent History of Real Estate

Real estate, like any market, has been prone to fluctuations. When looking at historical charts, these peaks and valleys seem to represent rather dramatic changes in value. Prices have gone up and then plummeted only to go back up again. This is the nature of the real estate market and it is hardly different from any other. The situation we find ourselves in today, however, is we are currently in the longest running low period in history.

The recent trouble started long before 2008. Real estate had always been a popular and generally profitable investment. Beginning at the end of the 1990s, there had been a huge surge in this type of investing. As the value of both developed properties and raw land began to rise, more investors jumped into the market. Houses were being purchased, land was being developed and inventories were decreasing.

In 2007 I attended a real estate investment event held by another investment group and I will never forget what I witnessed! First, they were teaching people to take HELOCs on their primary residence to by highly appreciating houses, which were significantly negatively cash-flowing each month. By significant I mean at least $500/mo. per property.

That certainly was enough to startle me, but what they taught next was insane...They taught that to make the negative cash-flow payments you could simply take HELOCs on the newly acquired houses as they appreciated. WHAT???? After they discussed this insane "investment" strategy and talked about a couple of areas in the country where these highly appreciating properties were located, they had them for sale that night.

To my astonishment, over half of the room got up and rushed to the tables set up to sell these overpriced houses. People were actually angry that they didn't have enough of them to go around. One lady who couldn't seem to get to the front, wadded up a deposit check and through it over the crowd to the sales agent behind the table. I'll never forget the frenzy I witnessed that night.

Investors were making a lot of money on paper but holding onto empty properties does little good. The goal, as with most investments, was to sell the assets while the prices were high. This meant there was a need for homebuyers.

Most ordinary people simply cannot afford to purchase a property in full. They will generally take out a loan from a bank, which, in this case, was a mortgage. Investors began selling off their properties at vastly increased prices and people were, for the most part, happy to purchase them.

In 2006, however, the housing prices peaked. As investors began to put their properties up for sale, the available inventory began to grow. There were eventually enough properties on the market that homebuyers were able to shop around while investors soon found themselves in a pricing war.

As is often the case with financial markets, this down turn in prices triggered a sell off on the part of many different investors. This further saturated the market with available properties. As the inventory of homes became ever more abundant, housing prices continued to drop.

This led to a chain reaction. Not only were the prices of empty houses dropping but the value of occupied homes began to drop as well. What this meant for homebuyers was they had essentially paid more for their home than it was currently worth. Adding to the mounting trouble was the emerging subprime mortgage crisis.

Ordinarily, a home buyer would need to qualify for a mortgage. The bank would assess their situation and then determine if they could afford to pay back the loan. To help fill the increased need for mortgages, they began lending money to people who would not otherwise qualify for such a large loan.

The rate of these subprime mortgages went from around 8% to 20% by 2006. What really sealed the fate of the housing market was the fact that 90% of these subprime mortgages had an adjustable interest rate.

As the values of homes and properties began to drop, the interest rate on many of these mortgages began to increase. The drop in value of the home made it impossible to refinance because there was no equity. The mortgage was more expensive than the home was worth and the monthly payments were more than the borrower could afford. This was a recipe for disaster and the bubble had begun to burst.

Home owners fell increasingly further behind on their payments which forced the banks to foreclose on the home. These foreclosed properties were then dumped onto the market at drastically reduced prices. Many of these homes were either brand new, or had been refurbished, and were located in desirable areas. The effect this had was of slashing the prices of non-foreclosed properties. Many investors saw their money melt away with alarming speed and began doing whatever they could to mitigate their losses.

What we find ourselves in today is the aftermath of this disastrous turn of events. There is plenty of speculation on who is to blame for this situation but the fact is this is the reality we are facing. In light of the recent history of the real estate market, it should be easy to see why most people would consider it a bad investment.

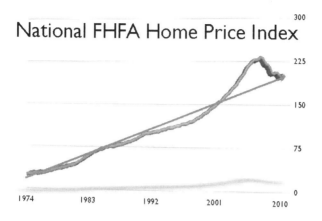

If we look at the charts, however, we can see the prices of real estate have gone up and down plenty of times. The peaks were high and the valleys were low. The only difference is our current valley is the longest in history.

What this says to me, as an investor, is that now is the best time to buy. The economy is desperate to get people buying property again. Banks are offering mortgages at historically low interest rates. There is plenty of inventory to choose from, much of which consists of beautiful properties located in great areas. Sellers are extremely motivated and are willing to accept a reduced price.

Historical Housing Starts

If we take into consideration the fact that properties values have always gone back up, it is hard to deny that real estate is possibly the best investment currently available.

The Different Types of Real Estate

Now that we understand what led to our current market climate, we should focus on the different types of real estate which investors purchase. For most people, real estate is a house. They generally only buy one and they do so through a real estate agent. In reality, however, real estate can consist of either developed properties, such as a home or business, or land. The differences between the two seem to be rather obvious but there are some subtle differences as well.

Houses

Houses are the most familiar type of real estate. Millions of people, all across the country, own a home and many of them consider it to be an investment. From an investor's point of view, however, your primary residence is not exactly an investment.

While it may be true that your home will grow equity and it may be possible to produce a profit by selling it, doing so requires you to move. When investors consider purchasing a home they do not intend to live in it but are looking to use it to produce either continued income or a large profit.

Houses are great income producing properties. An investor could, in theory, simply hold onto an empty home and sell it at a later date but this is not the best way to create a return. When you purchase a nice home in a desirable area, it should be relatively easy to find someone to occupy it. These tenants will then pay their rent on a monthly basis and this produces an income.

Over time, this monthly rent will have paid off much on the initial investment and the rest will be profit. This income is secure because, if the tenants refuse to pay, they can be evicted and replaced with new tenants who are more than happy to pay their rent.

This ability to produce a monthly income makes houses an attractive investment. A portfolio with a number of houses can produce many thousands of dollars a month in revenue. The biggest problem with houses, as we have seen recently, is they are very prone to market fluctuations.

Investors like stable and secure investments but the value of a house can drop significantly in a short period of time. In certain cases, the value of the house can drop so far there is no way to make a profit off of the investment. In a worst case scenario, investing in a house can actually cost an investor many thousands of dollars.

Another issue which needs to be considered is the idea that houses will depreciate in value over time. This is due more to the normal abuse a home receives from the elements and its own tenants than any fluctuations in the market. Homes need to be maintained and repaired on a regular basis and they will cease being brand new almost immediately.

The cost and hassle associated with this sort of upkeep can erode a bit of the profit which is available from this type of investment. There are, fortunately, a few different ways to avoid these problems and they will be detailed in the coming chapters.

Land

Land is a less familiar form of real estate because most ordinary people will have no use for it. Land actually comes in two basic forms. Raw land is exactly that, just a piece of the countryside which could be a field, a forest or even mountains and streams. Developed land, on the other hand, is usually located in developed and populated areas. The most obvious form of this type of real estate is an empty lot in a housing development, town or city.

Both raw and developed land has its benefits. Raw land can often be purchased for much less than developed land and it can be possible to purchase tens or even hundreds of acres for an incredible price. The problem with raw land, however, is that it can often be remote and therefore cut off from much of the necessary infrastructure needed to build anything. Not only might there not be any roads but there will be no access to utilities, such as gas and electricity. These will need to be installed which can cost quite a lot of money.

Developed land may cost a bit more than raw land but it has a great many advantages. To begin with, it is located in a populated area. This means it is a desirable chunk of land because it is the perfect location on which to build a home or business. In addition to this, it will likely already have access to local utilities and infrastructure which will save a significant amount of time and money if someone did want to build on it. This type of land is the most important element in building any type of property.

The greatest benefit this type of land has is it will almost always, without fail, appreciate in value. There is very little which needs to be maintained on a piece of blank property and the upkeep will generally amount to mowing the grass. As the surrounding area becomes increasingly more developed, demand for buildable land will increase at the same rate. If held for long enough, that piece of land may end up being the last available property, on which a structure can be built, within the confines of the town or city.

Unlike houses, however, land of both types will traditionally not produce an income. This is because there is simply not much which can be done with it short of building a house. There is no way to find tenants to occupy an empty lot, a business cannot be run on it and the land itself cannot be used for farming.

This is the common understanding of land but we have developed a great technique for using land to create a consistent and reliable income. This technique is so simple it is actually quite amazing that we do not see more investors doing the same thing. Our eye opening technique will be the subject of an upcoming chapter.

Notes

Notes are easily the least familiar type of real estate investment because many ordinary people simply have not heard of them. When someone takes out a loan, they have to sign a contract with the lender. This contract is essentially a promissory note, like an old fashioned IOU. It is a binding agreement between the borrower and the lender, one which can be enforced in court. The exact same thing happens when someone takes out a mortgage to purchase a piece of property.

Just like most loans, mortgages have collateral which is used to mitigate the risk of lending money to someone. If the borrower stops paying back the loan, the lender or bank has the right to foreclose on the property which was purchased with the loan. This property is then sold to recover the losses sustained when the loan fell apart. This is traditionally what happens and is the reason for the presence of foreclosed homes on the real estate market.

What many people do not realize, however, is the lender is not required to foreclose on the property. If they want, they can actually sell the note itself to recover the lost money. When this happens, the borrower's obligations, as well as the lender's legal rights, are transferred from the bank to the person who purchased the note. There are people who focus solely on purchasing these types of notes and have managed to make quite a lot of money.

The problem with notes is they are not exactly a real estate investment. The ideal goal in purchasing a note is to work with the borrower and help them start paying off the debt. Most people who invest in notes are not actually interested in owning the property, they simply want the monthly payments they receive from the borrower. Even though it is rarely done, however, notes can be used to take possession of a property.

Since the note holder is basically the bank, they have the right to foreclose on the property if the payments are not made. Notes initially enter the market as "non-performing" which means they are loans which are not being paid back. An investor could, in theory, purchase the note for much less than the value of the property, follow the required laws and then take possession of the property in the same way the bank would.

Our Favorites

All three of these items are viable options. They can be used to make a healthy return and are roughly equal in risk. What we, as a company, focus on is houses and developed land. Part of this is because we are big believers in sticking with what you know well.

Investing in notes can be tricky and there is a wealth of different laws and regulations governing every step of the process. Most of these laws change from state to state. Undeveloped, raw land is generally a bit useless due to its remoteness and the difficulty associated with getting it ready to be built upon.

Houses and developed land are simply easier to buy and trade. A home can be purchased and sold again almost instantly without doing much to it. Land, which is ready to be built upon, can easily be sold to a developer without the need to install utility access. Basically, there is so much less hassle associated with these two types of real estate that there does not seem to be much reason to bother with the others.

The most important reason, however, is these two types of real estate can be combined together to both mitigate the risks associated with either while creating a much higher return than would be possible with any one of them alone. This technique of combining houses and land is the basis of the Wealth Accelerator System.

Myths About Real Estate Investing

Despite the great profit potential associated with investing in real estate, most people are held back by fear. This fear is, more often than not, instigated by a number of common myths which are generally propagated by the media.

As we have mentioned, the media loves to sell bad news and it is what they do best. The problem is many people are missing out on wonderful opportunities because of these unfounded fears. This section will cover some of the most common myths related to investing in real estate and will illustrate why they are not true.

"Now is not the time."

This is probably the most common myth in our society today. Everyone has been hearing countless horror stories about people who have lost everything in the real estate market. These stories are coming from both investors and ordinary home owners so it is easy to see why they can make people afraid of real estate. As far as the guy on the street is concerned, real estate is finished and only a fool would invest in it. Perhaps, he would say, if the prices begin to rise you should consider investing in it again.

Even a cursory glance at the history of the real estate market will prove this myth to be untrue. The values of both homes and land have always fluctuated, this is their natural state. In fact, they have fluctuated dramatically two or three times every decade. When the prices are low people buy up the available properties. The inventory runs out so the values sky rocket. People begin selling off these properties and the prices eventually drop again.

What is different about our current situation is the values have not rebounded as quickly as they have in the past. We are currently in the longest slump in this market's history and many people believe this means real estate is no longer a viable investment option. Nothing could be further from the truth.

If we look at the statistics for things like population growth, particularly in certain areas, we can see it is continuing to grow at a very steady rate. Towns and cities are expanding further than ever before. More people are moving into these areas and they will need houses to live in and land on which to build these houses. As the population grows, the demand for real estate will increase. Since there is only so much real estate available, the value of these properties can only increase over time.

More importantly, the prices of both houses and land are incredibly low. A home which cost in excess of $250,000 only a few years ago can now be purchased for a fraction of that price. These houses are high value properties, located in desirable areas and many of them are either modern or refurbished.

Basically, these are houses in which people will want to live. The only reason they are so cheap is because their value is suffering along with the rest of the market. To add to this, many sellers are extremely motivated and will often accept even less than their asking price.

The economy needs people to purchase homes and build new properties in order to grow. There is a great desire on the part of both governments and large financial institutions to spur the purchasing of real estate. To help facilitate this, interest rates on loans and mortgages are at an all-time low. This means a mortgage for a particular home is incredibly affordable for those people who qualify for one.

When you couple the low prices of property with the cheap mortgages and combine this with the knowledge that property values have always rebounded, the fact that now is the perfect time to buy becomes readily apparent. Simply put, we are in an incredible buyer's market but this situation will not last forever. Once the prices start going back up, more people will enter into the market, driving prices even higher and an amazing opportunity may have been missed.

"Real estate is too risky."

This is another common objection many people have. Due to the recent problems in the real estate market, the risks associated with this type of investment have been blown out of proportion. Many people are afraid of entering the market because they fear losing the money they have worked their entire lives for. If you ask any armchair investor, they will say the risks associated with real estate make it a bad investment.

The truth is every investment comes with an element of risk. No matter what someone may invest in, the value of that asset could drop overnight. This is just as true for the stock market as it is for antiques and collectibles. Every investment, no matter how complicated or ordinary, carries with it some element of risk. It would be a lie to say investing in real estate is entirely risk free, the past few years have proven this.

What many of these armchair investors fail to understand is the amount of risk in an investment is often directly related to the amount of reward. One of the safest investments, if it can be called that, is placing money in a savings account. This account will offer a certain percentage of interest and there is almost no risk of it being lost. The problem with this is the return is so unbelievably small that it will almost assuredly be wiped out by inflation. The money may be safe in a savings account but it will certainly not produce a 40% annual return over ten years.

What really makes this myth untrue is it ignores any ability to mitigate the risks associated with a real estate investment. Simply purchasing a house and expecting to get rich from it will certainly carry a large amount of risk. There are so many factors at play that it is impossible to predict if this strategy will work.

What we do, however, is follow a strategy which creates an entire system. This system has checks and balances which help mitigate the risks associated with the investments. We use a variety of different techniques to cover ourselves in every step of the process. This system is exactly what you are reading about right now.

"You need to be an expert to make money."

I think it is safe to say that almost every person on the planet is interested in investing. When you tell someone that, instead of working day after day, they can use money to make even more money I find it hard to believe someone would not be interested.

Part of what holds people back from ever beginning to invest is they believe you need to be an expert. They understand financial markets are complicated and some, such as the stock market, can be exceedingly complicated at times. Most people simply do not know how to study graphs and charts or how to interpret changes in a market.

What many people are surprised to realize is a lot of them already know far more about investing in real estate than they imagine. Anyone who has ever looked for a home already understands precisely what makes a home valuable and desirable. They want a well maintained house, located in a nice neighborhood, close to amenities and good schools, one with a beautiful yard and a garage. What someone looks for when purchasing their own home is exactly the same as what makes any given piece of real estate valuable as an investment.

I will admit that investing in multiple properties is quite a bit different from purchasing your own primary residence. There are many things which need to be considered and managing everything gets more complicated with each property. The simple fact of the matter is real estate moguls will rarely know how to install a toilet, for example, and they are much less likely to actually do it themselves.

What they do is they hire experts. There are experts in every single facet of real estate investment and it is always possible to find someone who will lend their expertise in exchange for some money. You truly do not need to be an expert as long as you are willing to hire one when needed.

You also do not need to be an expert in real estate to make money like one. The only thing you need is a strong and reliable strategy which has been designed to mitigate risk and maximize profit. Fortunately, this type of system is precisely what this book is about.

Different Types of Real Estate Investing

Until now, we have been learning about the history of the real estate market, the myths surrounding it and the different types of properties investors will purchase. Now we will get to the interesting part which is how real estate investors generally make their money.

There are a number of different techniques which have traditionally been used to generate a profit from a piece of property. These techniques are relatively simple and are time tested methods of making money.

Flipping

What we call "Flipping" is a fairly simple concept. An investor will purchase a piece of property, whether it is a house or land, at a certain price and then sell it at a higher price. This is the most basic concept in investing and should be familiar to anyone who has ever heard of the stock market. Stocks are generally purchased at a certain price and then sold at a later time when the prices have gone up a certain percentage.

Property flipping works exactly the same way and the success of this technique is usually dependent on the state of the market. If property values are increasing rapidly, a profit can be made in a short period of time. When it comes to flipping, the shortest possible amount of time between the purchase and the sale is what investors are looking for.

The goal is not to own the property for an extended period of time but to sell it as quickly as possible at an increased price. This was one of the most popular methods of real estate investing during the boom of the late 1990s and early 2000s. Many people made a lot of money by doing little more than buying and selling.

In a slow market, one in which property values are either stagnant or rising very slowly, house flipping often falls out of favor. The reason for this is holding onto a property ties up an investor's money and they cannot use it until they have sold the house. If the values are not rising, there is no way to produce a profit.

One way to get around this is to occupy the house with tenants who will pay a monthly rent. While this will take some time to cover the investment cost, receiving this income is better than nothing at all. At this point, however, the investor has become a landlord and will have many things to deal with.

Rehabbing

You're not a true rehabber until your property makes it on the news!

At one of the many rehab and flipping boot camps I paid for years ago I heard a joke about rehabbers. They said rather "tongue in cheek" that you weren't a true rehabber until one of your properties ended up on the news. We all laughed and it was a fantastic line for the presenter. Fast forward three years…

I'll never forget the night I was watching the evening news and as they reported a homicide, just above the reporter on camera was my "$0 down – owner financing sign" 3 feet by 4 feet yellow with black letters. I called my brother (who was my partner) and we couldn't believe that we had finally made it in the rehab game. So, just remember, you're not a true rehabber until your property ends up on the news.

Rehabbing a property is another popular option which shares some similarities with flipping properties. The key difference is that rehabbing requires a bit more time and effort on the part of the investor. Using this technique, an investor will purchase a piece of property which needs some work done to it.

Houses are notorious for needing constant maintenance and many homeowners either do not have the money to keep up with it or lack the time and skills needed to do it themselves. As property falls further into disrepair, the value of it begins to drop. In some cases, a house may be so poorly maintained it has lost a significant amount of its original value.

This means it can be purchased for much less than what it would cost if the house was in pristine condition. A rehabber will purchase this sort of property and invest the money needed to repair it. They will add a new roof, fix the plumbing, manicure the lawn and improve the property in a number of different ways. They may also update the house by adding the new appliances and fixtures, which modern homebuyers are looking for.

All of these improvements begin to raise the value of the property. Given enough improvements, the value of the property may even exceed the price the original homeowner initially paid. Once the house has been fixed up and made desirable again, it is put back on the market for a price which exceeds both the cost to purchase the property as well as the cost to improve it. Doing this allows the investor to make a significant return because they have turned a troubled and neglected house into a home, which people will want to purchase.

Rehabbing properties can be a great investment strategy but there are still some complications associated with this technique. Finding and purchasing a poorly maintained property is not terribly difficult, there is at least one in every neighborhood. It starts getting complicated, however, when the actual rehabilitation begins.

The costs of labor and supplies can often be hard to predict and unexpected problems can arise. The real risk is in finding a buyer once the rehabilitation has been completed. Improving a house too much can create a situation where the home now costs far more than the surrounding properties and it can be hard to find a buyer.

Buy and Hold

"Buy and Hold" differs from the other techniques because it is more of a long term strategy. It relies on the value of a property increasing over time, even if this is an extended period of time. Due to certain social and economic factors, the value of many different things increases at a relatively steady rate. When it comes to property, this increase in value can be quite significant, particularly in a burgeoning and growing area.

An investor following this technique will do a fair amount of research before they spend any money. They are looking for areas which, they believe, will increase in value and desirability over time. Each investor will focus on a different time period and some may be considering decades' worth of growth. They will then locate a property in one of these areas and purchase it with the goal of holding onto it for that set period of time.

This strategy has a number of benefits, one of which being its ability to weather market volatility. Property values are guaranteed to fluctuate and there will be periods of both highs and lows. Since this is a long term strategy, there is no need to worry about such fluctuations because the investor can simply wait until the market rebounds before selling off the property. In addition, the property can be made to produce income during the waiting period by renting it out. Given enough time, the investment cost will be covered and the entire selling price will, in the end, be profit.

There are, however, also a number of disadvantages to this technique. Since this is such a long term investment, the money used to purchase it will be tied up for an extended period of time. Once the property is purchased, the money cannot be reinvested for a number of years. This makes it a poor choice for investors without large reserves of capital because only one investment property can be purchased.

This technique will also create a situation where the investor has now become a landlord and must take on all the related responsibilities. As people live in the house, it will inevitably need repairs and these can cost quite a bit of money. These costs will eat away at the rental income.

In a worst case scenario, the tenants can damage the property so severely it will cost many thousands of dollars to repair. Due to the amount of time required by this strategy, there is really no way to predict what sort of problems an investor will run into and there is no guarantee the value of the property will increase as hoped.

Our Strategy

Over the years I have tested a number of different real estate investment strategies. I have experienced both the benefits and problems associated with each one. During this time, I never stopped looking for ways to improve the traditional techniques. I knew there had to be a better way. Once I began to experience an increasing amount of success, I realized I had discovered the perfect strategy.

What makes our strategy different from the rest is that it is a more holistic approach to real estate investment. Rather than focusing solely on one technique or another, we decided to incorporate certain elements from each one. We developed a system which allowed us to use one technique to support another. This system allows us to enter into the real estate market while, at the same time, be able to mitigate a large amount of the risks generally associated with such an investment.

Using a unique and rather simple twist, I managed to find a better way to make money from real estate. This revelation was so powerful that not only did I drastically multiply my own personal wealth but I had the ability to teach it to others and watch them do the same thing.

This is a modern and proven technique for making a profit from real estate regardless of the current market conditions. I have used it to make money in booming, falling and even stagnant conditions. Most importantly, I have used it to help thousands of people do the exact same thing.

This strategy is exactly what you are about to learn right now.

Getting Rich ~~Quick~~ The Right Way

Income Producing Properties

Now that you understand some of the basics of real estate investment, it is time to focus on making money. This section will detail the specifics of income producing properties. You will learn what they are, how to find them and what constitutes the ideal property.

Properties, which can be made to produce an income, are wonderful investments. Not only are they a great real estate investment but they will begin paying you money almost immediately. More importantly, the rate of return on properties like this is much higher than with nearly any other type of investment. When done correctly, their total value will continue to increase over time. There have even been some instances where the value of the property multiplied within a few short years.

These properties are such a great investment, in fact, that Warren Buffet recently admitted he would purchase hundreds of thousands of single-family homes if he could manage them all. The most brilliant part about an income producing property is it can essentially pay for itself.

The income produced from the property can be put towards repaying the investment cost. Given enough time, the property will have paid for itself completely. When you consider the fact that these properties can be purchased with other people's money, in the form of loans and mortgages, they are almost free to begin with.

Different Types of Income Producing Properties

Properties which produce an income will come in a few different forms. Each one of these has its own advantages and disadvantages. The truth is there is no one property type which is better than another because they are all good as long as they produce an income. The difference, however, really lies in the difficulty associated with running and managing each property.

The simple fact is some of them are easier than others. In addition to this, some will cost more to run and maintain. Our goal is to find properties which have a low cost of maintenance which will allow us to put the majority of the income to better use.

Single-family Homes

A single-family home is easily the most basic type of income producing property. This is the traditional house which is occupied by either a single resident or a single-family. Properties such as this are generally found in suburban areas where the population density is not so high as to necessitate the use of multi-family homes. There are plenty of homes in more densely populated areas which were once single-family homes but were split up to accommodate multiple families. These, however, are not the same.

Everything in a single-family home is private and it will have all of the necessary equipment and utilities to support it. Many will have some property associated with them such as yards and will likely have their own driveway if not a garage. Depending on the location of the home, it might have its own well or septic system. Many single-family homes may also come with some sort of extra structure such as a shed, play set or even a storm shelter. The main theme is that a single-family home is meant for a single-family and will not have communal facilities directly associated with it.

Home such as this can come in a variety of different forms and may, in some cases, encompass large amounts of land as well. Single-family homes found in more rural areas will often come with an impressive amount of acreage while traditional suburban homes will generally have less than an acre of property. The amount of property associated with the home is important because it will affect both the amount of taxes and the cost of maintaining the property.

Finally, most single-family homes will not be attached to neighboring properties. There are, however, a few instances where a home such as this will share a wall with either one or both of its neighbors. Both attached and detached properties can be considered single-family homes as long as they can be purchased and owned separately.

One which is not attached to neighboring properties is often a better choice because there is risk associated with the neighboring properties. If, for example, the neighbors do not take care of their home and the pipes burst, the water can damage your property as well.

Example Property

Cashflow - $545/mo

- Purchase price = $100,000
- 25% down payment = $25,000
- Cashflow = $6,540 CROI = 26%
- Appreciation (5%) = $5,000
- Total = $11,540
- Annual return on investment (ROI) = *46%*

Duplexes

Duplexes differ from single-family homes in that they are traditionally meant to accommodate two separate residents or families. A real duplex will have been built with this purpose in mind and will consist of two complete apartments.

Each apartment will have its own bathrooms, kitchen, appliances and utilities connections. In most cases, a duplex will also have two separate entrances, one for each apartment. These entrances may be on different sides of the building or they could be right next to each other.

A duplex will generally have some sort of shared or communal areas. In certain locations, there will be one main entrance and a shared hallway which leads to individual entrances to each apartment. In duplexes with multiple floors you will often find a shared stairwell beyond the main entrance. Some will also share things such as porches, garages and yards. There will also likely only be one septic system or well, if applicable.

Traditionally speaking, the term "duplex" refers to a property meant for two families. In practice, however, this term is sometimes applied to properties meant for three or even four families. Even if the duplex can house more than two families, each one will be a complete apartment and there will also be some shared property.

In areas with an abundance of overly large and rather old houses, you will likely find many which have been converted to house multiple families. These are slightly different because they were not initially built to house so many separate people and so each apartment will be laid out in a different way. This type of property is also much more likely to have some sort of shared appliances or utilities such as laundry machines. For our purposes, we will not consider this sort of house as a duplex.

 **Example Property**

- Purchase price = $99,900
- 20% down payment = $20,000
- Cashflow = $7,200 CROI = 36%
- Appreciation (4%) = $4,480
- Total = $11,680
- Annual return on investment (ROI) = **58%**
- *Replacement Cost Equity = $150,000*

Commercial

Commercial properties differ mainly in use. These are properties which are meant to house some sort of business. This could be as simple as offices or as complex as a whole restaurant. What makes them great income producing properties is that the business should, in theory, be constantly producing revenue. If the business fails, it is often rather easy to find a new one to replace it. Commercial properties will generally be found in the commercial area of a town or city, rather than the residential areas of the suburbs.

When most people envision a commercial property they will likely think of a storefront. While this is a commercial property, there are also instances where a traditional home was converted to include either a storefront or office. This is most commonly seen with small and often personal businesses such as doctors, lawyers and accountants.

These are not people who need a large amount of space nor do they need commercial level utilities. More often than not, however, these properties have been rezoned and most areas will not allow someone to simply convert their own house into a business.

Commercial properties can vary quite a bit. A store, for example, may have little more than a large retail area, some storage in the back, an office and bathroom facilities, which lack showers. A restaurant or café, on the other hand, will need a significant amount of equipment to function properly. This could include a large kitchen with a walk in closet, ovens, stoves and dish washing equipment. This equipment is generally considered to be part of the property and is owned by the landlord.

Properties meant to house a business will also be subject to different laws and regulations than a residential property. According to laws such as the Americans with Disabilities Act, all commercial and retail locations need to be accessible to people with mobility restricting disabilities. Food service based properties will also need to comply with certain guidelines regarding the disposal of trash as well as noise level ordinances.

In some cases, a commercial property may also include a residential area. Many smaller commercial properties, such as small offices or even small restaurants, will have an apartment directly above them. This is generally used by the business owner to allow them to live on site. With certain properties, this apartment may have an entrance, which is separate from the business while others will not.

What Type Of Investment Should YOU Focus On?

While all of the property types mentioned above will produce an income, our system is going to focus on the single-family house. There are many reasons for this but the simplest explanation is these are the easiest to purchase, manage and occupy. A single-family home will only need one primary resident. This could be a single person, a couple or a whole family, the important thing is they can afford to pay the rent.

Since there is only one occupant to worry about, there is much less hassle when working with them. If the tenants move out, they only need to be replaced by another single tenant or family. A commercial property may only have one business but other businesses may have very specific criteria for what they need. This can make it hard to find another business to occupy the property in a short amount of time. During the time the property is not occupied it is costing you money.

The biggest reason we want to focus on single-family homes, however, is because we are going to use a "Buy and Hold" strategy. This is a property we are going to keep for a number of years in order to allow the value to appreciate while we collect the income. A single-family home is a much more stable investment and is more attractive to the type of tenants we want. Our ideal tenant is planning on occupying the property for as long as possible.

Generally, when someone rents a single-family home they are not renting a temporary residence. They have chosen the house because they want to make it their home and they plan on staying in it for a long time. Some people prefer to rent, rather than own, their home and they may stay in the same location for decades if possible. Since they are renting a home, rather than just a residence, they will also take more pride in its condition and will become members of the local community.

This is particularly true for families with children. There is a good chance the local school district was a big motivation for moving into the area. Their children will attend the schools, make friends and feel at home. At this point, the parents do not want to uproot their children and move them somewhere else.

The parents have become friends with the neighbors; they attend local functions and may even be a member of the local church. These things are all important to people and they will not give them up easily. What this means for us is this type of tenant will be very motivated to continue paying the rent and abiding by the rental agreement while occupying the property for a long period of time.

Duplexes and multi-family homes make it difficult to acquire this sort of tenant. The very nature of a duplex means the property is shared with at least one other person. This removes the feeling of having a private home in which a family can build a life.

Large houses, which were converted into multi-family homes, are even less attractive to our ideal tenants. These are often occupied by temporary residents, such as college students, and lower income families. In addition, many of these converted houses are found in more urban areas, which are also less desirable to our preferred tenants.

Where and How to Find a House

Now that we have established what type of house to look for, we need to figure out where to find them and how to determine if it is right for our investment strategy. This section will explain what to look for in an investment property and where they can most likely be found. Much of this information is easy to understand and will help you get into the right mindset.

A wise man once told me…"Live where you want to, invest where it makes sense!"

Your Own Backyard

The best place to begin looking for your first investment property is in your own town or city. There are a number of reasons for this but the primary one is that if you have lived there for a number of years you are likely an expert on the area.

You know which neighborhoods are the most desirable, where property values are rising, the location of the best amenities and the overall financial climate of the area. This is all priceless information and searching in your own local area can make things a lot easier.

Another benefit to this is the close proximity of the property. When you purchase a house and rent it out to an occupant, you will become the landlord and will be responsible for repairs and maintenance. More importantly, this property is an investment and you will want to make sure it is being taken care of. Keeping your investment property within close driving distance allows you to periodically stop by to check on it. When repairs are needed, you will be able to oversee them yourself.

Out of State

A house in close proximity to your own, however, is not a requirement. There are wonderful houses available all over the country and it can be a good idea to search in other states as well. One reason for this is that some towns and cities are experiencing a boom and are growing rapidly.

While the town you live in may be nice, it might not be growing and expanding as rapidly as other areas. Finding, purchasing and managing properties in far off states is actually simpler than it sounds. The only thing that is needed is a reliable team of people to help you. This will be explained in detail shortly.

Important Considerations

There are a number of important factors to consider when searching for houses to purchase. While the value and condition of the house are important, certain factors will contribute more to your success in finding stable and reliable tenants. These are the factors which make a certain area a desirable location in which to live. Fundamentally, they are the same factors you would search for when looking for your own primary residence.

Economic Factors

Economic factors are always an important consideration and they refer mostly to the local economy. One of the best indicators of a good area in which to invest is that of job growth. The ideal house will be located in an area which is experiencing steady and positive job growth.

This means the local businesses and industries are expanding, new businesses are moving in and jobs are being created. Wherever there are jobs being created, there will be people moving to that area. This positive job growth will almost guarantee a steady influx of new residents who are all looking for a nice place to live.

The rate of commercial development is another important factor. This refers to the creation of both new businesses as well as the construction of new locations for these businesses. This sort of development could take the form of new shopping malls, new major retailers and even the creation of new locations for small businesses.

In addition to this, the renovation and updating of existing commercial properties is also a good sign. The growth and expansion of commercial properties is wonderful because it is a great indication of both job growth and population growth.

Positive population growth is a perfect indicator of a good location. This means people are moving into the area and the population is increasing. This is important for a few reasons. Primarily, positive population growth means people are moving to the area and are looking for housing. It is also important, however, because people will be needed to fill the jobs being created and to spend money at the newly developed commercial locations. People are the most important element in any economy and without them it will fail. Negative population growth, as should be obvious, is as big a warning sign as you can hope to find.

Schools and Universities

The presence of schools and universities is also something to keep in mind. Schools are important to families and these will often be one of the biggest factors in their decision to move to a certain area. It is actually quite common for families to move for no other reason than to ensure their children are attending the best schools possible.

The quality of the schools is equally as important as their existence. It can be a great idea to take a look at the statistics for the schools in the area and make sure they are adequately funded, receive good reports from the state and have a high graduation and college acceptance rate.

Universities and colleges can also be a great indicator of a good area. The presence of a respected and well known university will often almost guarantee that an area is both desirable and a great place in which to invest. College towns will also have their own unique personality due the presence of so many young people.

These types of towns often have very active local economies and will receive a healthy stream of money from out of town sources. The arts are also an important part of most college towns and theaters, galleries and museums will often be well funded.

These are all things which can help make an area desirable.

Health Care

Adequate health care facilities are another important factor. Nearly every area will have access to local doctors and dentists but many will not have their own hospital. Some may have small or underfunded hospitals that can be just as bad. When people, particularly growing families, move to an area, they want to make sure there is access to well-funded and complete health care facilities.

They will also want to make sure these facilities are not terribly far away. When looking at different areas, you should check to see how far away the nearest hospital is. It can also be a good idea to do a bit of research on the local hospitals to ensure they are well regarded.

Health care facilities can also be a good indicator of other factors as well. Large hospitals need adequate funding and enough trained professionals to make sure they are run correctly. Many of these employees will be people like doctors and surgeons who will generally live in more affluent neighborhoods. The lower level positions employ people from a range of economic strata and will help keep the local population employed and able to afford housing.

Crime Rates

It should be obvious that a low crime rate will go hand in hand with a desirable area. The statistics for different crimes are generally public information and can usually be found on the internet. It is important to consider both the instances and types of crimes as well as the crime per capita. Crime per capita basically refers to the number of certain crimes committed each year compared to the number of people living in the area. An area may have a low number of annual assaults, for example, but a low population number will mean a higher chance of being assaulted.

One thing to pay attention to is steadily or rapidly declining crime rates. Crime is generally inversely related to the quality of the area and its local economy. As the economy begins to rise, crime levels will often begin to decrease. This is due to a number of different reasons and there is no point in speculating on them now.

What is important is that a quickly declining crime rate can sometimes mean property values will soon go up. If a property is purchased early on, the potential increase in value can be staggering when the area has been cleaned up.

What to Buy

Knowing what to buy is just as important as knowing where to buy. The specific houses we want for our system will follow a certain set of criteria. These rules are not exactly set in stone and may vary a bit from location to location. Knowing what sort of property to look for, however, can certainly make the search that much easier.

Positive Cash Flow

When we look for a house, one of the most important factors is positive cash flow. What this essentially means is the income generated from the house will exceed the costs associated with maintaining it.

Every house will have a number of regular costs, including things like repairs as well as taxes and utilities. All of these expenses need to be paid on a regular basis and the money will, according our system, come from the income the property produces. You do not want to purchase a house which has a level or negative cash flow because it will either not make you any money or actually cost you money to own.

Positive cash flow can be estimated with a little research. Once a property has been chosen as a candidate, it is important to find out how much it will cost to own it on a continued basis. You should find out how much the taxes are, what the utilities costs are generally like and how much routine maintenance will need to be done.

It is also important to factor in any expenses which may arise at some point in the future. Some things, such as septic systems and appliances, will eventually need to be replaced. Since we are using a long-term "Buy and Hold" strategy, some of these costs may be inevitable.

Once the costs have been calculated, an estimated monthly rent should be determined. A general idea of how much this rent will be can be found by looking at similar rental properties in the area. The estimated costs should be subtracted from the estimated revenue on both a monthly and yearly basis. If there is still money left over, after all of the costs, then there is positive cash flow potential in that property.

Rent Ready

When we purchase a house we want to rent it out as quickly as possible. As was mentioned previously, every month that a property goes unoccupied it is costing you money. There will likely be a number of homes available for purchase in every area but some of them may not be ready to rent out immediately. There are plenty of homes that are slightly older and will need some updating. Some may need mild repairs while others might need major repairs such as a new roof.

The goal is to be able to do as little as possible to get the house ready to rent. We are not looking for a property that needs renovation. We do not want to replace anything major. If we can avoid it, we do not even want to paint or refinish the floors. One or two of these things may be unavoidable and, in fact, doing some small improvements can increase the potential rent. The important thing to remember is that any major repairs or improvements will be coming out of your pocket and will increase the initial investment costs.

Affordability

Price is always a factor for both buyers and renters. You want to find a house which is affordable and within your budget. It should be comparable in price to similar properties that are in roughly the same condition. It can be tempting to purchase a large, expensive property in the hopes of collecting a much higher monthly rent but this is almost always a mistake.

The reason for this is affordability. As a factor in choosing a rental property, this also refers to the cost of the rent. The monthly rent, which the tenant needs to pay, has to be within their own budget. You have to take into consideration their income and financial obligations.

A family which has two children and a car loan and makes $60,000 a year will only realistically be able to afford a certain level of monthly rent. Some people are simply not good with their personal finances and they may agree to pay a rent which is beyond their means. This will guarantee trouble in the future because they may begin to miss payments as they are forced to choose between different obligations.

The cost to invest in the property will affect the cost of the rent. This is why it is important to find a house which is affordable and comparable to the local average. Paying far too much for a house will require you to charge far too much in rent to recover the costs. In addition, if the rent for your property is much higher than the local average it can be hard to find tenants to occupy it. This is particularly true if there are other houses for rent which are roughly the same as your own.

Reliable Property Management Companies

This is one thing which many first time investors neglect when looking for properties. Many people think they will be able to save some money by managing the property themselves. The problem with this is they fail to realize how much work is involved.

As a landlord, you will be responsible for a variety of different things. If the toilet leaks, the sink stops draining or an appliance breaks down you will have to fix or replace it. This sort of problem is fairly common, especially in a house with a family, and many people quickly find it frustrating and time consuming to keep up with.

A reliable property management company is a real estate investor's best friend. They are the people who make sure everything is taken care of and they do most of the work for you. More importantly, their maintenance and repair people are usually experienced professionals and will do the job right the first time. There is, of course, some cost associated with hiring a property management company but the amount of time and money they save makes them a vital part of our system.

It is, however, important to make sure this company is reliable and has been around long enough to have plenty of experience. There are a number of methods, which can be used to find a company like this, and the internet is a great resource. Before hiring the company, it can be a good idea to check with the Better Business Bureau and other websites, which allow customers to post reviews. It can also be a great idea to contact other property owners to find out what they think of the company.

It is vital to make sure the company operates in the area in which your house is located. In order to be truly reliable, they must be able to respond quickly. A close proximity to the property will help make sure this is always the case.

Investor Concentration

We are purchasing houses for two reasons. We want immediate cash flow and future appreciation. When you look at a specific area, we need to consider the investor concentration of that area. What this refers to is basically the amount of properties that are rental properties owned by real estate investors like yourself. The concentration of these properties in any area will always affect the appreciation of a property and the amount of money that will be made when it is finally sold.

Before buying anything, you need to know the number of rental properties compared to the number of owned properties. This is especially true for houses located in a development. If more than half of the houses are rental properties that are owned by investors, then it is not a location in which real homeowners are buying. The investors who own these properties will eventually put them up for sale and, as we have seen in the past few years, an overly abundant inventory of comparable houses can destroy the appreciated value.

To put it simply, you want to invest in a house that is located in an area predominantly populated by real homeowners. These are people who purchase and occupy their own primary residence. A high concentration of this type of property is indicative of an area in which people want to live. This is a neighborhood in which people want to buy a house. When you finally put your house on the market, there will be people wanting to buy it.

Your Ideal House

At this point, you know how to identify a good area in which to invest and have developed a basic idea about the type of houses to purchase. This section will describe, in detail, the criteria for an ideal investment property. This house is perfect for somebody who is just entering into the world of real estate investing but it is also a great option for anyone with more experience as well.

Single-family or Small Multi-Family

Single-family homes, as described previously, are the perfect place to start investing in real estate. They are easy to purchase, finance and manage and they are incredibly abundant. Single-family homes are the perfect place for our ideal tenants which make them the perfect choice for beginners and experts alike. In the near future, as the economy continues to rebound, the demand for this type of real estate will increase. This creates a situation where the value of the property will steadily appreciate during which time the pool of available renters will grow.

Small multi-family homes are also a great place to start. Two to four families is the ideal range for an investment property and this is why duplexes can be a great entry level property. As was said before, however, houses with multiple occupants do carry their own set of problems. Managing and occupying one of these properties will be quite different from a single-family home. Despite these drawbacks, there are still a few distinct advantages to a multi-family property and anyone looking for something slightly more involved will do well with a two to four family property.

Newer is Better

Be careful. A few years ago I was talking to one of my clients who had questions about an advertisement they received from a competing company. I'd seen this too many times before and this time I had to "show" what was wrong with the property for sale. This property was in Kansas City (nothing wrong with my hometown) and was a horrible investment. I had a trip to KC planned so I told the investor that I would video the area so he could see why I warned him.

His jaw dropped when I can back with a video of several boarded up houses and graffiti on houses and businesses in the block surrounding that investment property. Just because a property is cheap, doesn't make it a good investment. Just because the picture of the house looks cute, doesn't mean the neighborhood is nice.

The ideal investment property will also have been built fairly recently. This is a relative concept and, in some cases, a twenty year old home may be the newest one available. As a general rule, the newer a house is the better it is as an investment.

Newer houses will have a much longer life span, which is an important element in our long-term strategy. Everything about it, from the foundation to the roof, will be relatively new and modern. This removes a lot of the risk associated with purchasing an older home and will help save time and money down the road.

As you search for properties, you may come across a few which were built a century ago. These older homes can often be quite large and beautiful but they are typically very awful investments. The older a home is, the more likely it will be full of hidden problems.

An old home may appear to be in good condition but there are problems brewing in the walls, under the floors and in the structure itself. In addition to this, old homes are notoriously hard to heat and cool, which will affect the affordability of the rent for your tenants.

3 Bedrooms, 2 Bathrooms, Attached Garage

This is a fairly typical single-family house and there is a good reason for it. As anyone who has a family can attest, there simply has to be multiple bedrooms and at least two bathrooms. This is the type of property a family will look for and they are one of our ideal tenants.

The three bedrooms offer people the ability to give each child their own room, have a guest bedroom or even use the extra room for another purpose. The garage offers security for their vehicles and a place to store certain items. These are also some of the most popular types of houses. When it comes time to finally put it on the market, this house will receive quite a bit of attention.

This, however, is not a hard and fast rule. Potential investment properties can have slightly more or slightly less than this. In some areas, having four or five bedrooms is the standard because people generally have larger families. For the same reason, two bedrooms and one and a half bathrooms might be normal.

The important thing to remember is that it needs to fit our investment strategy and is affordable both for you and the tenant. Purchasing the only house in the area with six bedrooms and four bathrooms is probably not the best idea.

1,200 Square Foot Minimum

This applies mostly to single-family homes. The minimum size for an investment property should be 1,200 square feet. Anything smaller than 1,200 square feet is likely to be too small for a family, particularly one with children who are a bit older. When you consider the number of rooms in most houses, you can see that anything smaller than this will result in very cramped and confined spaces.

The modern trend is for open floor plans and spacious rooms so this cramped layout will affect the desirability of the house. In the case of multi-family homes and town homes, it might be acceptable to purchase one that is slightly smaller but it is important not to go far below this minimum size.

Rent Ready

The ideal house has to be rent ready. We do not want to sink any more money into it than we have to. Whether or not a house is rent ready is determined by a number of factors. The ideal house should have a well-maintained yard with bushes and trees which were recently trimmed. If there is a pool then it should not need repairs or cleaning.

Ideally, the appliances should be included and in good working order. The walls should not need paint and the floors should be finished. Blinds should be in the windows and light bulbs should be in every socket. Our ideal investment property is one that a renter can move into the day after we take possession.

What to Avoid

Understanding what constitutes the perfect property is good but it can be equally as helpful to know what to avoid. Knowing what not to buy will narrow down your search while helping you dodge a truly toxic real estate investment. It should be obvious, at this point, that there are quite a few warning signs to watch out for and these are just a few:

Falling Property Values

Plummeting property values were fairly common right after the bubble first burst. Today, however, we are past this declining period and have been steadily stagnant for a few years. If property values are still dropping in a certain area then this is a warning sign. There are plenty of reasons the values may be falling and it can be impossible to predict them all. The only thing you need to know is these values are not likely to go back up any time soon.

Loss of Major Industry

There are plenty of towns and cities that grew around a major industry. This industry provided employment for the local population who, in turn, supported the local economy. When this industry is the main employer in the area, its loss can have devastating effects on the local property values. The best example of this problem is Detroit.

Abundant Inventory of Homes

Basic economic theory tells us the value of a good is related to the abundance of that good in the market.

When there are too many homes available for purchase, the value of each one will fall. If that area is not experiencing a population boom, these houses will likely go unsold for quite a bit of time. They may, one day, increase in value but that could be decades in the future.

Replacement Cost Equity

Replacement cost equity can be a bit tricky to understand in the technical sense. The specifics are not terribly important to us, at this time, but a general understanding of the concept is helpful. There are basically two different ways to own a house. Someone can go to a real estate agent, look at available properties and purchase one.

The other option is to purchase some land, hire an architect, hire contractors and build a house from scratch. There is a cost associated with each option and they are not always the same. Building a house is complicated and there are a number of different expenses that need to be considered. When everything is calculated, the current cost for building a home is roughly $75 - $100 per square foot.

The cost to build a specific house is something you should keep in mind when looking for properties to purchase. Once you have found the square footage of a house, you can estimate what it might cost to build that exact same house. For example, a 1,500 square foot house would cost between $112,500 and $150,000 to build.

The next thing you should do is compare that estimated building cost with the asking price for the house. There are plenty of cases where the cost to purchase that house is actually much less than it would be to build the same house from the ground up. That same 1,500 square foot house might, for example, be priced at $100,000. This is $12,500 to $50,000 less than it would cost to build. Think about that for a second.

It costs less to buy the house than it would to build it or replace it.

This is important because it means the house is undervalued. It is worth more than it is being sold for because it would cost more to build the same structure. When you can get a house for less than the building costs, as long as the area is good, you can be fairly certain there will be future appreciation in the value of that property.

Simply put, we should not be able to purchase a house for less than its replacement cost. The only reason we are able to do this is because the entire housing market is currently undervalued. This is, however, only a temporary situation. It will not last forever. As soon as people begin to realize how much appreciation is inherent in these houses, they will start buying again. When they do, we will no longer be able to pay so little for a house.

There is no way to tell when this will happen but we can be sure it will happen soon. It will not be long before the rest of the country wakes up and realizes they can purchase these houses for less than they are worth. As soon as this happens, values will rise and more people will enter the market. The ability to purchase undervalued houses like these will disappear.

What this tells us is now is absolutely the best time to buy these properties. There may never be another time when we will be able to get such an incredible deal on houses which people will, very soon, be looking to move into. Once everyone realizes this is the case, the opportunity will be over. You are fortunate to be entering into the real estate market during this time but you have to act now and start buying up these properties before it is too late.

Land

Until now we have been talking about purchasing houses. A piece of property with a house built onto it is, arguably, about as developed as a parcel of land can get. This parcel started life as raw land, it was developed and then a house was built on top of it.

This chapter is going to focus on the actual land itself. Land is my absolute favorite investment. Now you are about to learn why it is so great and how to find the perfect parcel of land in which to invest.

The Advantages of Land

Land has a number of advantages over other types of real estate investments. Many of these are inherent in the nature of land itself while others are due to the market and the way in which it fluctuates. This is not to say land is a better investment than a house, only that land makes a wonderful companion to the other types of real estate investments.

It Almost Always Appreciates

One of the biggest advantages to land, from an investment standpoint, is it almost always appreciates in value. Land is a hard asset. It is something which will always be needed and which cannot be duplicated. Every parcel of land is unique and no two will ever be exactly the same. It is also the most important part of real estate development because without it there can be no houses.

Land appreciates in two different ways. It will appreciate in value over time at a relatively slow but steady pace. It will also, however, appreciate quickly as the market goes up. When the surrounding property values are rising, the value of land in that area will also rise. Due to the need for land during real estate booms, it will often rise farther, relatively speaking, than houses in the same area.

The important thing to remember is land is almost always more affordable than fully developed property in the same area. A parcel of land could be located right next to a house. Both of them can be appreciating quickly but the land will always have a much lower price. What makes land great is the percentage of the increase, meaning the percentage of return on the initial investment, will go up at the same rate as the house right next to it.

What really sets land apart from houses, in terms of a real estate investment, is that this tendency to appreciate over time is part of its nature. Houses, on the other hand, will tend to depreciate over time because of the nature of their creation. When a house is built and then occupied, it will slowly begin to fall apart and need a number of repairs.

Given enough time, a house will need to be almost completely renovated to both fix problems and accommodate the needs of a modern occupant. A house which was built in 1900, for example, has needed to be renovated a number of times. Not only did it need the usual upkeep but it needed to accommodate electrical wiring, access to phone lines and eventually access to the internet.

Land, however, does not need any of this. There is generally nothing more to land than dirt and foliage.

Even when that land has been developed, as can be found in many housing communities, there is very little which needs to be done to keep it up to date.

Certain types of houses may fall out of fashion but land will always be needed and it will always be desirable. People will generally want to purchase a modern home which makes older homes tough to sell. Land is the same today as it was a century ago and it never falls out of fashion.

There is a Limited Supply

No matter what someone may invest in, a limited supply usually denotes a good investment. When something can be multiplied it can flood the market and cause values to drop. Land is the epitome of a limited supply. There is only so much land on the planet and once it is all bought up there will be no more. This is one of the reasons land makes such a great investment.

Land in a desirable area is even more limited. Most towns and cities will have borders. Some of these borders will be drawn on a map. Other borders have to do with distance and proximity. A town can be desirable for a number of reasons, one of which can be the availability of employment. At a certain distance, it is no longer viable to rely on that town for employment due to the length of the commute.

The closer a parcel of land is to the center of desirability, the rarer it will be. This is due to development and the growth of the local area. As more people move to this town there will be more houses built. These houses will take up land and new houses will need empty lots on which to build. In most towns and cities, there is an extremely limited supply of buildable land.

This all combines to make land a very powerful investment. You could, in theory, purchase a parcel of land in a town. That town will experience a boom and development will skyrocket. As you hold onto this piece of blank property, it may eventually become the last piece of buildable land in the area. Once you sell it off and someone builds a house, there will be no more land available. This is the definition of a limited supply.

There are No Tenant Hassles

We touched on this a bit in the last chapter but there are a number of hassles associated with rental properties. Things will go wrong from time to time. Roofs will leak, appliances will break and repairs will be needed. As a landlord, all of these are your responsibility. Things can be made a bit easier by using a property management company but it can still be a hassle.

On top of the common problems with owning a house, dealing with tenants can often be frustrating. There really is no way to tell what type of a person someone truly is. Tenants have been known to stop paying rent, rent out portions of a house and even refuse to leave. These problems can be solved but not without wasting time and money.

Land, obviously, has absolutely no tenant problems at all. It is simply an empty parcel of land, ideally in a nice area. There is no need to look for tenants, sign rental agreements or even hire a management company. Land will just sit there, quietly appreciating in value until you are ready to do something with it. It is almost entirely passive and this makes it a wonderful addition to your portfolio.

Getting Rich ~~Quick~~ The Right Way

John Jacob Astor: A Brief History Lesson

The power of land as a real estate investment can be clearly seen by a quick examination of history. John Jacob Astor is a name which is likely familiar to many people. The reason for this is he was America's first multi-millionaire. While he made much of his initial money from a variety of business ventures, it was real estate that really set him apart.

Toward the end of the 18th century, Manhattan was an important port and a bustling area. It was not, however, the vast metropolis we know today. The main concentration of the population was located around the southern tip which is where most of the docks and industry were located. Everything north of the southern tip of Manhattan was still fairly rural.

John Jacob Astor began purchasing real estate in these less developed areas of Manhattan. He did this because he knew the area would grow. The island of Manhattan is surprisingly small and there was a very limited amount of real estate available. One of the properties he purchased was a farm that covered an area from what is now Broadway, west to the Hudson River and which stretched from 42nd street to 46th street. Most of this area is now known as Times Square.

Later in his life, John Jacob Astor was being interviewed and he was asked if he had any regrets. This is what he said:

"If I could live all over again, I would buy every square inch of Manhattan."

Not only does this story illustrate the power of investing in land, this specific quote illustrates how important it is to take action while the opportunity is still available. Realistically, John Jacob Astor probably had very few regrets about the amount of money he had.

What he did know, however, was there would never be another opportunity like that again. Manhattan is home to some of the most expensive real estate in the entire country. It is also one of the most developed and densely populated cities in the world. John Jacob Astor took advantage of an opportunity and essentially purchased Times Square when it was still farmland.

Land Banking

The story of John Jacob Astor is the perfect example of what we call "Land Banking". Some people will consider this as real estate speculation but there really is a key difference. Astor did not purchase properties and hope they would appreciate in value. He did his research, looked at the population growth, as well as the amount of space available, and made an educated decision.

He knew the population would continue to grow and, as it did, so would the need to develop the surrounding land. At the time, it was difficult to get to areas like Brooklyn and Queens and so the development would happen in the limited space of Manhattan Island. The land he purchased was just beyond what was currently being developed but perfectly situated for future demand.

This is basically the definition of land banking. It is where you find a city which is experiencing growth, determine the direction in which it is physically expanding and then purchase property in the path of this growth. In a short period of time, the value of this land will go through the roof as buildable land becomes increasingly scarce.

How It Is Done

The concept of land banking is fairly straightforward and so is the process by which it is done. The first step is to locate an expanding and growing city. Cities such as Boston, Chicago and New York may have experienced the majority of their expansion over a century ago. Cities like Salt Lake, however, are experiencing growth right now. As soon as the economy begins to rebound, this expansion will accelerate.

Determining Past Expansion

The first thing to do is look at the recent history of the city. You only need to go back about 50 years. Looking at a map of the city, it will be easy to see where the city ends and the outlying areas begin. When you compare this old map to a modern one, you will be able to see the directions in which it is expanding. We can even draw a circle around this city to better define it.

Determining Future Expansion

Determining future expansion is relatively easy. There will be a few natural features which may limit growth in some areas. Builders will always choose the easiest properties on which to build. This means they will likely avoid difficult terrain such as mountains and swamps. Manmade features, such as interstates and highways, as well as shopping malls and industrial centers will also determine the growth pattern.

The goal is to figure out the direction in which the city is expanding. These are areas which are, currently, lightly developed. They could be rural farmlands or sparsely populated suburban areas. Using our map, with the circle denoting the current borders of the city, we can draw another circle that encompasses the areas of future development. These are our target areas.

Purchasing Land

Now that you have an idea of the general area in which you should purchase land, it is time to look closely at the area. In these outlying areas, which are so close to the city, there will likely be some development already happening. Much of this development may come in the form of housing communities but there may also be the creation of new commercial centers as well.

The ideal pieces of land, for our system, are those that have already been developed to the point of being ready to build. These are parcels of land that have been cleared, leveled, and have access to the infrastructure needed to build a house. This sort of land can often be found within these housing communities.

The people who build these communities will purchase a large section of raw land. They will develop the land and begin building a few houses on it. They will not, generally, build houses on every available lot and some will be kept blank. These lots will become hot commodities as the city expands into these areas and buildable land becomes increasingly scarce.

Land banking works by purchasing lots such as these and holding onto them as the city expands. As was mentioned before, land is virtually a passive investment and there is very little which must be done while it is held. There will be taxes that need to be paid but, other than that, there really are no other expenses. This land is basically money in the bank.

The city will continue to expand. When the economy rebounds, this expansion will accelerate exponentially. As that happens, the value of the land will increase at the same rate as the surrounding real estate, whether it has a house on it or not. The land will appreciate to many times what you paid for it while you let it sit there and hardly think about it. When the time comes, you sell this land and collect the profit.

Getting Rich ~~Quick~~ The Right Way

Why Now?

We are currently living in the middle of an interesting situation. When John Jacob Astor purchased the farm on Times Square, there had been very little development in the area. We, on the other hand, are living in a time directly after an incredible boom.

During this boom, real estate development was rampant. There were new communities being developed all over the country. Land was being improved and made ready to build. Houses were being built on this land and the market was full of people purchasing land and building on it. All of this was done because people thought the boom would last forever.

The problem was that the bubble burst. Suddenly there was a huge overabundance of developed property and no one was buying. The prices plummeted and most of the development stopped. This is where we are now and it is a wonderful time to start purchasing again. We know the crash has stopped and we have leveled out.

More importantly, the cost of these developed parcels of land is at an all-time low. This land is the ideal investment because it is absolutely build ready. There is nothing that needs to be done to it. The most beautiful aspect of this type of real estate is that you can currently get it at raw land prices. This means you can get a build ready lot for the same price as a chunk of remote wilderness.

The prices on these lots have been low for a few years now. What makes today different from the past is that cities are overdeveloped. They have done as much as they can with the space they currently have. The only thing they can do now is expand into the outlying areas, the same areas where buildable lots are currently so cheap.

This means the appreciation of these lots is simply a matter of time. The city is forced to expand and, as it does, it will begin consuming the buildable land. This increases the scarcity of this type of property and increases the value at an impressive rate. In just a few short years, these lots will be worth so much more money that people will be wishing they had invested early.

Now is the perfect time to start buying these lots because we are so incredibly close to this economic rebound. There may not even be another two years' worth of time before we are seeing an increase in property values and an increase in both development and expansion. The fact that you can purchase a build-ready lot for the price of raw land is, in all honesty, simply insane.

What this says to an investor, however, is the market will recognize how incredible this is. When it does, the time will have run out. As soon as people realize they can purchase land that is ready to build and located right in the path of future expansion, for pennies on the dollar, the inventory will be gone in a few short months.

What we have right now is an opportunity like that which made John Jacob Astor the country's first multi-millionaire. This is incredible and there is absolutely no way this will last for much longer. There will simply never be another chance to purchase property with this type of profit potential within our lifetime.

If I could convince you to do one thing it would be to take advantage of this opportunity right now.

Getting Rich ~~Quick~~ The Right Way

Combining Houses with Land

The previous chapters in this book have covered the two main forms of real estate investment. Purchasing properties that create an immediate monthly income and land which will appreciate in value are both sound investments. Both of these can be used to increase your own personal wealth and there is a great potential for profit in each one.

The problem we have with this is it is how real estate investing has been done for centuries. This is not exactly secret information and you may even be familiar with some of it already. When I first started with real estate I followed the old model. I did things the way they had always been done. I made money but I did not make as much as I felt I could.

I was limiting myself because I had not yet discovered a better way. As I became more familiar with the industry, I realized I was losing out on a lot of money. On top of that, I was often in a position where one major problem could actually destroy my entire investment. I was facing the same exact fears, which keep many people from investing in real estate at all.

Over the course of a few years, I began to develop a new system. This system not only increased the amount of money I made but it also shortened the amount of time I needed to make that money. After a few tweaks and improvements, I also found a way to help mitigate a lot of the risks associated with my investments. The most surprising fact I discovered is that most people simply are not doing things the way we are.

This was surprising because my system is actually very simple. I had not, at first, thought I discovered anything new. It seemed so obvious to me, based on my past experience, that I was sure other people had come to the same conclusions.

As I talked with a variety of people, however, I found out my system was unique. Most people were only following the conventional method and I want to explain this method before I show you what makes my system so much better.

The Conventional Method

This method is arguably as old as real estate itself. It is essentially the most basic and straightforward way of investing in physical property. To be completely honest, it is a perfectly good way to make money from real estate. This is the first method most people learn and it is the easiest to understand. There are only a few steps to this method:

Purchase a House

The first step is to do a bit of research and locate a house that is for sale. There are a number of different criteria which people use to find these houses. Most people will look for properties that follow the rules we outlined in the chapter on income producing properties. Some people, however, intend to spend a little bit of money fixing up the property.

The main thing they are looking for is a house that can be rented out. It needs to be affordable, according to their budget, so they know they will eventually make a profit from the monthly income.

This sort of budgeting is different for each investor but most rental properties will fall into a certain range of prices.

Some of these properties may be duplexes or other forms of multi-family properties because this will allow them to increase the amount of monthly income they receive. Some investors will have a bit more money to spend and might even purchase more expensive commercial real estate. No matter what type of property they purchase, the goal is to rent it out.

Find a Tenant

The next step is to find a tenant to occupy the property. This can be as simple as finding one person to occupy a house or as complex as finding a business which will be able to use the space. Renters can be found in a number of different ways. Ads can be placed in newspapers, information can be posted on websites and, in some cases, a third party can be used to locate the renters.

There are sometimes a few hidden costs with this step. It can often cost a bit of money to publish an ad in a newspaper and some websites might require a membership fee. One cost that many people neglect to plan for is the rental agreement. This contract is incredibly important and absolutely must be used when renting out a property. Most people will hire a lawyer to write it for them.

Once the tenant has signed the rental agreement, they are ready to move in. As a general rule, the tenant is responsible for the rent as soon as they sign the agreement. Many people will require the first month's rent up front and will also require a security deposit. This deposit is usually equivalent to one month's rent.

Pay Off the House

Once the property has been purchased and a tenant moves in, the investor will begin receiving a monthly income. A portion of this income should be put towards a property management company. Some of it may also be collected as profit and put in the bank. Most of the revenue, however, will be used to pay down the cost of the house.

Investors will generally take out a loan to purchase their investment properties. This can be a great idea because it allows you to use other people's money to create an income producing investment. Even if they paid for the house in full, however, they will still need to recover the investment cost before they are actually making a profit.

This can be a great strategy because the house will begin to pay for itself. As the rent comes in each month, the investment cost is being paid down. If everything has been calculated correctly, the entire house can be paid off within about 10 to 15 years. After it has been paid off, the property can either be sold or held in order to continue collecting income.

The Fatal Flaw

This can be a successful strategy for making money from real estate and it has been used for many decades. There is, however, one fatal flow with this method. Houses are prone to problems. It is only a matter of time before something goes wrong with it. As a general rule, there are certain things that eventually need to be replaced such as roofs and fixtures. On top of this, there is the constant potential for problems with plumbing, wiring and appliances.

To make matters worse, there is always the threat of some sort of disaster. No matter how careful someone may be in choosing their investment properties, there is at least a small chance of one natural disaster or another. These disasters, such as floods, tornados and earthquakes, can completely destroy a house. There is also always the potential for certain individual disasters such as fires and other accidents.

The problem with this method lies in the way the money flows. Most people will charge a certain amount of rent that is basically equal to the monthly costs to own the house. The rent will go towards regular maintenance and the paying down of the initial investment. This leaves them with no buffer what so ever. If anything goes wrong, the costs will come out of their pockets.

If something goes wrong with the house, the investor is faced with a tough decision. They can use some of the rent to pay for the repairs but this leaves them paying for the monthly cost of the house out of pocket. The other option is to pay for the repairs out of pocket but this cost needs to be factored back into the overhead. If anything goes wrong, the profit will be impacted and the time to pay off the property will be extended.

Even if nothing goes wrong with the house itself, something can still go wrong with the tenant. There is no telling what might happen with a tenant but we can be sure that the loss of a tenant means the loss of the monthly income. It could take a month or two to find a new tenant and, during this time, the costs are coming out of the investor's own money. Once again, there is no buffer.

OUR Wealth Acceleration Method

Part of what makes our method so great is it offers you a buffer. Rather than focusing on one individual investment, we focus on a couple of investments that can all support each other. If anything goes wrong with one of them, we have a safety net to fall back on. In addition to this added risk mitigation, we can also shorten the amount of time needed to pay off the properties.

Our method is fairly simple to understand. At this point, you should understand both investing in rental properties and developed yet empty plots of land. These are the two pillars on which our system is built. They create a firm foundation that will support a continually growing and expanding system of wealth generation. Our method starts the same way as the conventional method.

Purchase a House

The first step in our system is to purchase a house. This house should abide by all of the criteria outlined in previous chapters. We want a modern, rent ready property which is 1,200 square feet or larger. It is important to ensure the house is rent ready and not in need of any repairs. The faster we can rent it out, the better.

This house can be a single-family home or a multi-family dwelling such as a duplex. As we have said, the more complex properties have their own benefits and drawbacks. We do, as a company, own a few commercial properties but for the purposes of this book we will not worry about them. The main theme with this step is simplicity. We want something that is basically ready to go as soon as we are.

Once everything is ready, we want to rent out the house. This should be fairly easy and if the house is rentable it should not take much time. It is, however, important to remember things such as the rental agreement and the need for a property management company. The property manager will add to the simplicity of the system while the agreement will cover us in a number of ways.

As we begin to collect the monthly rent, we will put it towards the cost of the house. This is similar to the conventional method in that we use the house to pay for itself. Some of the money will go to the property manager and the cost of regular maintenance. Most of it, however, will be paying down the cost of the house.

Purchase Land

This next part is where our system begins to diverge from the conventional method of real estate investment. What we want to do is purchase one or two lots that can be used to help buttress our rental property investment. The land we buy does not have to be in the same area as the rental property but doing this can helps keep things simple.

The type of land we want was described earlier. This is where the land banking comes into play. What we really want from these parcels of land is future appreciation of value. While the land may not be producing an income, we are watching its value increase. As it increases, it will begin to reach our sell off price. This is similar to stock market investing when someone will have an exit price on a given stock.

You really do not, however, need to have a set value at which to sell off the land. If the values are quickly rising then there is no reason to lose out on the money that can be gained by waiting a few more months. As long as you keep an eye on both the value of your property and the trends for the surrounding area, you will know what to do.

Sell the Land

We have actually had several of our clients sell their lots over the past few years. One in particular stands out as he sold 3 of his for 6 times what he paid for them within 1.5 years of buying them. Net profit on the sale of all 3 was $49,500. Others have sold to the neighbor who wanted to own a larger lot.

If we have done our research correctly, our land should have experienced a significant increase in value. Our general time frame for this appreciation is about 5 to 10 years. In an ideal situation, the land has increased to many times what we have initially paid for it. At this point, we want to sell it off to the highest bidder.

Depending on how much the land is worth, you could stand to make many tens of thousands of dollars on the land alone. In some cases, the value of the land may be much higher than this. The point is we want to make as much money from selling this land as possible because we are about to put it to immediate use.

Pay Off the House

Now that we have sold off our parcels of land, we are flush with available capital. Rather than simply keeping this money as a profit, we are going to reinvest it into our system. At this step we will use the money made from the land to pay off the house. Since we are dealing with about a 5 to 10 year timeframe, the amount of money needed to pay off the house should be a bit less than when we started.

If we were very smart with our land investments, we might be able to pay off the house completely. This is why we often suggest purchasing at least two parcels of land. Land will appreciate quickly but it is generally priced less than an average house. Owning multiple pieces of appreciating land, however, will likely earn us enough money to completely cover the cost of the investment in the rental property.

Monthly Profit

Even though we have paid off the house, we still have a tenant living in it. This tenant is still paying us the monthly rent. Since the house is completely paid off, however, almost all of this income is profit. There are, of course, still the costs of the property management company and the necessary repairs to consider but these are rather small.

Using the conventional method we may have had to wait 15 or 20 years to get to this position. Depending on the cost of the house, we might have had to wait even longer. Since our system uses quickly appreciating land to supplement the costs of the house, however, we have managed to pay it off in a fraction of that time.

This is part of what makes our system so powerful. While we will stand to make a good deal more money, when all is said and done, we will also make that money much faster. While other investors are still waiting to pay off their rental properties, we are sitting back and collecting profit. Ten years later, while the conventional investors are still waiting, we have made a truly impressive amount of money.

The Result?

Free & Clear in 10 Years

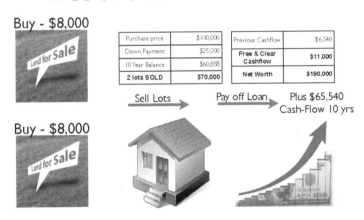

Buy - $8,000

Buy - $8,000

Purchase price	$100,000		Previous Cashflow	$6,540
Down Payment	$25,000		Free & Clear Cashflow	$11,000
10 Year Balance	$60,858			
2 lots SOLD	$70,000		Net Worth	$190,000

Sell Lots → Pay off Loan → Plus $65,540 Cash-Flow 10 yrs

Reinvest

This is the greatest step in the system. This is what causes our system to drastically accelerate both the rate of wealth accumulation and the speed with which it is acquired. At this point, we find ourselves in a situation in which we own a rental property that is delivering profit on a monthly basis. We could, if we wanted, just save this money or spend it on vacations and nice cars.

What we are going to do, however, is reinvest this money. We are going to repeat the previous steps in order to build an entire wealth generating system. We want to purchase another rental property, find a tenant and begin collecting our monthly rent. If possible, we want this property to be close to the other so we can use the same property management company.

The difference is we are able to use the income generated from our first property to help pay off the second. Now we have a situation where the monthly rent, which is being spent to pay down the house, is actually doubled. This would cut the time needed to pay off the new property in half if we were going to follow the conventional method.

What we are going to do, instead, is purchase a few more parcels of land. We will hold onto this land for about 5 to 10 years and let it quietly appreciate. At this point in the process, we have one rental property that is paid off completely, one which is being paid off by two different income sources, and a few pieces of blank land which we rarely need to think about.

Once this land has appreciated enough, we are going to sell it off like we did before. Once again, we are flush with available capital. We are going to spend some of it on paying off our second rental property. Since we have been using the income from both rental properties to help pay it off, however, we will only need to use a much smaller percentage of our land profits.

Now we have some profit left over from the land sales as well as two rental properties that are delivering us nothing but profit every month. Following this simple system, we have managed to create a system that is bringing us more money than ever before. Imagine, for a second, if we were to continue following this system in the same way.

Eventually we would have a number of different rental properties. Each one will be paid off and the monthly income will be mostly profit. At a certain point, we will be receiving so much money from these rental properties that we will be able to pay off a new house in no time at all. Every fully paid off property we add into our system reduces the amount of time needed to pay off a new property.

If we continue to invest in land at the same time, we will need less and less of the land profits to pay off the new house. This means every time we sell off our parcels of land, we are collecting a greater percentage of profit than before. Every time we repeat the cycle, we are making more profit.

You do not need to be a financial expert to understand how amazing this is. We are creating a system that will, after only a few cycles, begin to pay for itself. If we continue to follow this method, we will essentially not be paying anything for our new rental properties. We will be receiving so much money, from both the monthly income and the land profits, we will be able to pay off a new house almost immediately.

This is exactly the system we have used to generate millions of dollars in revenue. It is also the exact same system we have used to help others do the same thing. We have followed this system for many years and enjoyed a tremendous amount of success. I, however, am the type of person who is always looking for ways to improve what he does.

I was looking for a way to increase the profit production of this system. I wanted to find a way to make my money faster so I would be able to reinvest it faster. I eventually realized what I could do to increase the benefits of this system. It was such a small tweak, with such a great payoff, that I almost slapped myself for not thinking of it before.

Supercharging the System

The ability to make a lot of money from real estate is no secret. Even if they do not know how it works, many people know real estate is a great investment. We discussed some of the fears that keep people from investing in it but there is another reason some people never enter the market. They simply cannot afford the entrance fee.

Real estate is not the cheapest investment someone can find. The initial costs can often be a bit more than an ordinary budget can really afford. The fact is, people want to buy land but they often do not have the money to purchase it. I had always known this but one day something clicked. I had finally found the secret to improving my already successful system.

According to our strategy, we purchase parcels of blank property and hold onto them for a number of years. We are forced to wait until we sell our land to collect any money. This works perfectly well but it does require us to wait until the property has appreciated. What I figured out was a way to produce income from this blank land while we held onto it.

What we want to do is purchase land as we always have. These are great pieces of property and they increase in desirability over time. After a couple of years of continued appreciation, the number of people interested in purchasing the property will increase. We do not want to sell off the property too early but we can offer to let someone purchase it incrementally.

The solution to supercharging our wealth generating system was to sell some of our land to other people on a financing plan. They would purchase this land in much the same way as they might purchase a house. They will make monthly payments on the property and, after a number of years, will completely own it. The payments will have been calculated to take the future value of the land into account.

This means we will decide on a length of time for the payment plan. We might, for example, intend to have the buyer pay off the land within 5 years. We will then look at the rate of appreciation on the land and calculate its value in 5 years. Using this information, we formulate a financing plan that allows us to get the same amount of money when the deal is done.

What makes this different, however, is we will begin getting that money right away. Rather than waiting for years to unlock that capital, we can use it to start paying off our rental properties right away. Ordinarily this land would just be sitting there but this technique turns it into an income producing property as well. This little trick makes it so every property you own is producing income and supporting the system.

In addition to that, you have broadened the pool of people to which you can sell your property. Following our original system, we had to rely on people with the full amount of money. Allowing people to purchase land on a payment plan, however, means almost anyone with a little extra money can be a potential buyer.

People who otherwise could not afford to purchase land will have access to this opportunity. You will be making money every month rather than waiting. It really is a win-win situation for everyone involved.

When I realized how beneficial this is to each side of the equation, I knew I had found what I was looking for.

The absolute best part of it is that this portion of the system is entirely optional. The original method works perfectly well and it improves with each repeated cycle. Selling land to people, with a financing plan, only increases the speed of the system. You could even do this with only part of your properties. If you purchase two parcels of land, for example, you could hold onto one and finance the other.

This makes our system incredibly dynamic and able to adapt to the different needs of every investor. There are really very few investment strategies that are pliable in any way at all. Most of them require a strict adherence to the system. Our system, on the other hand, lets you do whatever works best for you. No matter which route you choose, you will be making incredible amounts of money.

Getting Rich ~~Quick~~ The Right Way

Wrapping Up

This book has covered quite a lot of information. At this point you have gone from someone who was interested in making more money with their investments to someone who understands how to do exactly that. Purchasing income-producing properties allows us to begin making money right away. Supporting this property investment with capital appreciating land will not only help reduce risk but will speed up the process.

We have covered what types of properties to look for as well as what to avoid. You have also learned the precise criteria we use to find the absolute best investments in both rental properties and developed land. This has empowered you to begin doing your own research. You should, hopefully, have an idea of the types of properties you would like to purchase.

By now you should understand our system and why it is so great. Rather than waiting for decades to enjoy the profits of an investment, our system allows you to begin multiplying your wealth almost immediately. This truly is the best way to both plan for retirement and create a situation where money is no longer a concern that keeps you up at night.

The one thing this book has yet to cover is how to find the money to begin investing. Some people may have been smart with their finances. They have cut down on their expenses and put a few dollars away whenever possible. If they have done everything correctly, people like this may already have the money needed to begin.

Other people, however, represent a more typical example of our current situation. No matter how much money someone may earn every year, it can be nearly impossible to put any money away. The costs of living, coupled with other normal expenses, can easily use up most of a person's available capital. These people are not bad with money, they simply do not have a great excess of it.

This chapter will outline a few different methods that can be used to acquire the initial investment capital. These methods are fairly simple and have been used by people, just like you, for many years. Most of these can be handled on your own but an accountant can often be a helpful ally. This final bit of knowledge is the last key you will need to begin earning more money than you ever thought possible.

Where to Find the Money to Invest

Every investor understands the fact that money can be used to make more money. This is what makes investing such an intriguing prospect. Rather than working, day after day, for a set amount of money, smart investments can produce many times the amount of financial resources generated by working. One thing that keeps many people out of the world of investing is an absence of the needed capital to begin.

What many people are surprised to find out, however, is they often have money that is either not doing a thing or is not earning as much as it could. Most of the time, this money can be found in one sort of retirement account or another. An employer often sets up these retirement accounts and many people have them.

IRA

Many people begin retirement planning long before they will need to worry about it. One of the most common methods of doing this is an IRA. An IRA is an Individual Retirement Account and can either be set up by an employer or by the person themselves. Money is placed into the IRA, which is then invested, in a variety of different things.

The goal is to increase the overall value of the IRA through smart investments. These investments are made by someone else, often with little input from the account holder. Every IRA will have some sort of regulations regarding how much money can be contributed and when it can be removed. An IRA can also consist of either pre-tax or post-tax contributions.

This can be a great way to begin saving for retirement but there are a few problems with this technique. Due to the recent down turn in nearly every sector of the economy, most IRAs have lost a significant portion of their value. This is because they have focused on traditional investments such as stocks. This is typical of most IRAs because these investments are generally considered rather safe.

The most important thing to keep in mind, however, is the account holder has very little control over how the money is spent. Custodians of an IRA are not allowed to give out advice and will usually follow their own investment strategy. These investments can often pay off but they will require an extended period of time.

This money is, essentially, sitting in an account and not making you as much as it could. There will be penalties and taxes associated with removing the funds before a certain date which means the money cannot simply be removed and reinvested elsewhere. The best way to get around this problem is to set up a Self Directed IRA

SDIRA

A self-directed IRA is like a traditional IRA with one key difference. Rather than contributing money to a fund and allowing a custodian to invest it, an SDIRA allows you to make your own investments. While a traditional IRA will likely consist of traditional investments, an SDIRA can invest in almost anything including real estate.

More importantly, the money located in a traditional IRA can be moved into a self-directed IRA without incurring any penalties. This means the entirety of a retirement account can be placed into a different account without paying taxes. Now that you have control over how the investments are made, you can use that money to purchase real estate without the need to worry about losing it to fees, taxes and penalties.

The profits made from these SDIRA investments are put back into the account. They can then be invested again to produce even more money. You may not be able to take this money out of the account and spend it, without incurring fees, but you will have the ability to use it to follow our system.

Switching your funds to an SDIRA can be a great way to find the money needed to begin investing. It will also allow you to increase your retirement fund much faster than with traditional options.

401(k)

A few years ago, I met with a couple that had been caught in the economic downturn. They had been frugal for their entire lives and had saved what was a great amount for their retirement. All of a sudden it was cut in half through no fault of their own. As we discussed their goals and were able to look at where their assets were and how much they had, we quickly ascertained that they could retire if they invested in real estate. I remember the look on their faces as I told them that they would still be able to make it happen. I'm not sure they believed it then, but they do now. They own several income producing properties and they are waiting for the market to turn to sell their land to pay off mortgages. 401k's are powerful when invested in real estate.

A 401(k) is another type of retirement fund. This is one of the most common types of retirement funds and many people have one. The money placed into a 401(k) is "tax deferred" which means it is not taxed until the money is removed from the account. Traditionally, the contributions for the 401(k) are deducted from an employee's paycheck, before taxes are taken out.

Many employers offer a 401(k) plan where they will match the employee's contribution up to a certain point. This can be a wonderful option because an employer is essentially paying you to save for retirement. In some cases, the employer's contribution can be quite significant and far more money can be added to the account than would otherwise be possible.

The problem with a 401(k), however, is that this money is tied up in the account for a number of years. Most 401(k) plans will have a list of different penalties that someone will incur if they withdraw money from the account. These penalties will often be removed once the person has reached a certain age. This is generally about 60 years old, at which point someone can begin removing their money.

It is important to read the fine print on your 401(k), if you have one. Depending on your age, you may already be able to withdraw a certain portion of the funds to reinvest. The only problem is this money will then be taxed and you will lose a certain portion of it. Overall, though, investing this money is a better option.

One thing many people are not told, however, is they may be able to take out a loan from their 401(k). In this situation, someone is basically borrowing money from their own account. A loan agreement is drawn up and an interest rate is set for the repayment of the loan. The beautiful part of this is the interest payments are then added back into the account.

When you take out a loan from a bank, you are paying them to use the money. When you take out a loan from your 401(k), however, you are paying yourself. Not only are you able to use a certain portion of the 401(k) funds, but you will have more money in the account, when the loan is repaid, than you would otherwise have had.

Using this simple little trick, we could take out a loan from our 401(k). We could then invest that money into our system. Since our system begins generating an income almost immediately, we can begin repaying the loan. Once everything is finished, we will have our income producing properties as well as a 401(k) that now has all of the original funds plus the interest fees. We have just made money by issuing a loan to ourselves.

Home Equity Loans

Home equity is another thing that can be leveraged to produce the necessary investment capital. When someone purchases a house, even if it is a primary residence, they are hoping it will appreciate in value over time. This appreciation is essentially profit because the house is now worth more than what they paid for it. After a certain amount of time, the home may be worth tens of thousands more than it was originally worth.

This excess money is referred to as equity. This equity is what makes a home valuable, from the standpoint of a homeowner. Traditionally, the problem with this is the house needs to be sold before that money can be used. It is locked up in the home until the point at which the house is sold and the homeowner moves out.

A home equity loan, however, is something that can be used to unlock this money today. It is often referred to as a second mortgage because it is a loan that uses the house as collateral. A loan is granted, based on the appreciated value of the home. It is paid off in increments with interest applied to each month's payment.

Depending on the value of your own home, you may be able to receive a loan that amounts to hundreds of thousands of dollars. You are not selling your home and are still able to live in it. If we take this money and invest it in our system, we will begin generating an income. This income is used to pay off the home equity loan. Once the loan is paid off, we are back to where we started.

This is another technique to essentially get free money to invest in real estate. There will be some money lost on the interest payments but this is one of the best ways to find the initial investment capital for our system. Rather than letting this money sit around, a home equity loan lets us put our own money to work for us today.

Traditional Loans

Traditional loans are another way to find investment capital. These loans are typical mortgages and many people are already familiar with how they work. Someone will first need to qualify for the loan. Part of this qualification is stating and explaining how the money will be used. The rest of it is ensuring the person will be able to pay back the loan.

Once the loan is granted, the money is then spent to purchase a house. Payments on the loan must be made every month and there will be interest applied to each one. Loans such as these can have terms that are as long as 20 or 30 years. The loan itself is secured by the property that was purchased with it.

If you qualify for a traditional loan, this can be a wonderful way to get started. Our system is designed to create income-producing properties. What this means is the money needed to repay the loan does not come out of pocket. The money comes from the investment. This allows you to use someone else's money to purchase a property that will then pay for itself.

There is one more piece of information that makes this a great option. Due to the crisis in the housing market, banks are trying to encourage people to purchase homes. One way in which they are doing this is by offering historically low interest rates. There has never been a time when you could take out a mortgage with such a comparatively low interest rate.

Using a traditional loan, we will receive all of the money we need to begin. The payments from the rental properties will go towards paying off the loan. Given enough time, the house you purchased has paid for itself and you are clear of the debt. With such low interest rates, this option costs less than it has in a very long time. Once the loan has been paid off, you have basically purchased the property for nothing.

Asset Liquidation

Many people have been investing in a variety of ways for a number of years. The most traditional way in which people invest is to purchase stocks but many will also invest in currency markets and other non-traditional options. These are assets and they are worth money.

In some cases, people will have a portfolio of long-term investments. These could be a number of stocks that they intend to hold onto for a set period of time. These stocks are appreciating in value but that money cannot be used until the stocks are sold. Some stocks will produce dividends but these payments are always rather low. They are, in fact, significantly lower than what can be made with our system.

Rather than keeping so much money tied up in slowly performing, long-term investments, these assets can be sold. Selling them now may mean they will produce less money than if they were sold in ten years but that money can be put to better and more immediate use. Liquidating some available assets can be a great way to find yourself flush with available capital.

Stocks, however, are not the only type of asset that can be liquidated. Many people collect a variety of different things. These can be as small as baseball cards or as large as cars. Most collectors will understand their respective markets and will focus on valuable and desirable items. These items will have, hopefully, appreciated in value.

In addition to collectibles, things such as jewelry and recreational vehicles can also be sold. Many people may have a car that they use on a daily basis and a boat or motorcycle which they use recreationally. Since these items are not vital to their continued success, selling them can be a great idea.

Since our system is going to be making us quite a lot of money, in a short period of time, delaying some gratification can really pay off. By liquidating a number of different assets, you will have the money to begin purchasing properties that produce an income. After a short period of time, all of that money will have been returned to you and you can either reinvest it or spend it on acquiring more of the same assets.

Government Funding

The government is just as concerned about the economy as everyone else. They understand that growth needs to be encouraged to help the economy rebound. Part of this manifests itself in the form of government loans and grants. This is money that the government will give to people to help spur the development of certain areas.

There is a great variety of different government programs. Depending on where your properties will be and what will be done with them, you may be eligible for government funding. This can be enough money to get started. What makes this sort of money really great, however, is that it often does not need to be repaid.

Not everyone will qualify for this sort of money but it can be a great source of capital. It will allow you to essentially use free money to begin acquiring your own wealth. In addition to this, you are actually helping local economies as well as providing homes for people who need them. It is important to do some research to find out what kind of programs there are and whether or not you qualify for them.

Other Methods

The methods listed in this chapter are all wonderful ways of finding the money needed to begin investing in real estate. The lack of available capital is the main reason so many people never get into investing at all. They simply believe they cannot afford to start purchasing properties, even though they understand how profitable this can be.

One thing we love to do is show people the different ways in which they can get their hands on this capital. Nearly everyone we talk to has access to money they did not even know about. More often than not, this money is simply sitting around and waiting to be used. We call on a variety of different experts to help people identify these resources.

No matter who you are or what you do for a living, there is at least one thing you can do to generate investment capital. There are simply so many different options that it is nearly impossible to fail at finding one which works. The chances are good, if you are reading this book, that there is money you could be using.

One of the keys to our success, as a company, has been working closely with our clients and students. We have worked with many thousands of people and have successfully helped them get started building a system which dramatically increases their wealth. If you feel as though none of these capital-generating methods apply to you, contact us.

We know all of the tricks, we have done this many times in the past. We want you to become financially independent and live the life you have worked so hard to enjoy. Our team of experts will work with you, one on one, to determine where your investment capital will come from and how to get it. Even if you have no clue about finances, we will help you find the money you need.

How We Do It

This book has detailed every specific piece of information you need to understand our system. You now know everything needed to begin accumulating your own wealth and building your resources for the future. This should be an exciting time. This is the point in your life where you finally begin to make the money you need to support the life you want.

Real estate investing is relatively straightforward. There are countless books and videos that cover this subject. Our system can be applied to a great variety of different properties found all over the country. When followed correctly, our system will begin to make you money regardless of the properties and locations you choose.

At this point you have all of the knowledge needed to go out and begin purchasing real estate. What you do not have, however, is a team of people which will help make this happen. When we began creating this system, we realized we wanted to give our students more than just information. We wanted to work with them, to help them achieve the same success we have.

This is what makes our system different. Not only do we offer all of the information you need, we offer our own personal experience and expertise as well. This is not just a book. It is an invitation for you to come work with us. We want to be there for you, to show you how our system works in the real world. Our company has been created around this mission.

What We Do

What we do as a company is provide the final piece of the puzzle. Our goal is to bridge the gap between education and implementation. There are plenty of other courses out there. Some of them may even provide valuable information. The problem is, once the course is over, students are left on their own without any expert help.

Our company exists, in part, to carry students from the educational phase to the actual, real world, implementation phase. First, we provide you with the information you need. Once the education is finished, we will literally hold your hand as we take the first steps toward financial independence. We do not want our students to make that first leap alone; we want to be there with them.

We want to develop a personal relationship with you, one that allows us to understand your situation and present the absolute best properties for you to purchase. There is no guesswork involved. The plan we follow is personally tailored to your goals and needs. Some of our competitors have laughed at this but we are not here to simply sell information, we are here to help you.

How We Work With You

The first thing we do is understand your situation. Everyone will begin this journey from a different place in their lives. Some may have been planning for retirement for decades while others may just be getting started. We know there is no single, universal solution to everyone's financial worries. This is why the first thing we do is provide a thorough, free, personal assessment.

This assessment will take everything into account. We will determine your current situation, your available resources and how much money can be allocated to this system. This is all collected into an in depth and personalized report on your current financial status that we will go over with you. This is a one on one experience and you can be sure all of our information is accurate and true.

The next step is to develop a personalized wealth plan. This is essentially our own proven system but tweaked and customized to fit you and you alone. The plan we give you is your own plan, based on your personalized assessment. It is designed to work as perfectly as possible for you, your needs and your desires. You will not need to guess or experience the frustration of trial and error.

We will sit down with you and personally go over your plan. You will be able to, instantly, see how it follows our system and how it has been customized for you. This plan is basically a map that shows you how to get from where you are now to where you want to be in just a few short years. People have paid thousands of dollars for a personalized system such as this and they still do not get the continued personal relationship and dedication that we offer.

Once we have assessed your situation and created your plan, it will be time to look at properties. This is another step that you do not have to take alone. We have a vast portfolio of available properties and we will filter it according to your personal criteria. Rather than sifting through thousands of listings, we will only show you those properties that are ideal for your wealth accumulating strategy.

Our portfolio consists of a great variety of different properties. They have all been chosen because they fit our system perfectly. Each one is located in a prime area for appreciation, one that is incredibly desirable to renters and owners alike. These areas are ready for staggering growth over the next few years. Every property we show you will be a great investment geared towards your own needs.

Even after you have purchased your first few properties, we will not abandon you. Your properties may be located in different areas and they will require regular upkeep. This book has already detailed the importance of finding a reliable property management company. Rather than leaving you to find one on your own, we will set it up for you.

We will essentially do all of the work to ensure that your investment properties are ready to go. There really is very little you need to do other than choosing your properties with our help. We pick them out, explain them and then make sure they are taken care of. All of the guesswork and risk is eliminated. We provide everything you need to get started right away.

Investing in real estate is never completely passive. There is, in reality, no such thing as a passive "turn key" investment. What we have done, however, is make real estate investing as simple and easy as possible. Real estate may never be entirely passive but we have worked hard to make it as streamlined and worry free as we can. This book has provided information and our company provides the implementation. With this book and our help you have everything, from start to finish.

Who We Work With

Over the years, we have worked with people from all walks of life. Many of our clients have been between the ages of 40 and 65. These are people who are close to retirement and are beginning to worry about their financial future. Many of these people had been saving for retirement and lost much of their assets to the recent problems in the market. We like working with these people because retirement is quickly becoming a reality for them and they are motivated to make it work.

We have also, however, worked with plenty of clients who were younger. Retirement planning is something that should be done as soon as possible. The earlier someone begins planning for their retirement, the sooner it will happen. Younger people are great clients because they have seen what has happened to many of the older generations and they want to avoid these issues in their own lives.

Business owners are also wonderful clients. They already understand the need to reinvest in a successful financial strategy. They can approach things with a business mindset and truly understand the value in each step of our system. On top of this, they often have the resources needed to get started and might be able to merge their own businesses with their investments.

Some of our clients were simply ordinary people who work hard, day after day. These are people who live in a two-income household. They have children and bills, obligations that make their existing financial assets incredibly precious. They know they need to be smart with their money and they are concerned with always taking the proper steps.

Our clients are often not people of great financial means. They receive the majority of their income from their jobs and they have worked with the same company for many years. Ideally, they have begun taking advantage of benefits offered by their employers such as a matching 401(k) plan. These people are dedicated, hardworking and willing to save for the future.

The bottom line is we will work with anyone. The only requirements we have are a willingness to work for your own dreams and the dedication needed to continue following the system. Our ideal client is someone who wants to break free of their current bonds and live a life of financial independence. We are willing to work hard for you and the only thing we ask is that you are willing to work with us. If you have ever thought about retirement and wondered if it will happen then you are the type of person we want to work with.

Why Us

We will admit there are other systems out there. We cannot speak to their credibility but there must be a few which will work. We, however, offer something that these other options do not. When you work with us you are receiving a complete system. Everything from financial assessments to property management is included.

What we offer is an opportunity to tap into something that has been continually making people significant amounts of money for many years. This is something that has already been set up, it is ready to start making you money, the only thing you need to do is accept our help. This is essentially a gold mine and all you need to do is start digging.

We are not a clearinghouse of properties and we do not exist simply to make money from our clients. We work so closely with you because your success truly is our objective. Money is not something we worry too much about. After following this system for so many years, we have more money than we know what to do with. What we really want is to help people like you attain the dream of financial independence.

This is what makes us so different. We are dedicated to you and your success. This dedication is why we want to work so closely with our clients. You can, of course, simply follow our system on your own. You can do all of the research yourself, try to customize the system on your own. You can take on all of the risk and learn from your mistakes. We are simply here to make sure you are successful. That is all we truly want to do.

Contact Us

We love to hear from our clients and students. There is no question too simple or too complex, we will answer every one of them. If there is ever any bit of information that you need help with, do not hesitate to ask. We are available any time you need us and will always be able to schedule a time that is convenient for you.

There is no cost to contact us. We do not expect you to agree to anything. We are simply extending our help as a part of the overall system this book has presented.

Contact us today and find out for yourself what makes us so different.

Wealth Accelerator System
2975 W Executive Parkway, Ste 137
Lehi, Utah 84043
1-800-991-5311
GetStartedInvestingNow.com

5114455R00079

Made in the USA
San Bernardino, CA
23 October 2013